ATHANASIUS (From an ancient MS.)

The Church History Series

V

ATHANASIUS

His Life and Life-Work

BY

HENRY ROBERT REYNOLDS, D.D.

*Fellow of University College, London, President of Cheshunt College,
Author of "The Exposition of and Introduction to St John's Gospel,"
"Pulpit Commentary," "The Philosophy of Prayer," etc, etc*

'Thomas answered and said unto Him, My Lord and my God '—JOHN xx 28
'This was the plain condition of those times, the whole world against Athanasius, and Athanasius against it, half a hundred years spent in doubtful trial which of the two in the end would prevail, the side which had all, or else the part which had no friend but God and Death, the one a defender of his innocency, the other a finisher of all his troubles '—RICHARD HOOKER, *Ecclesiastical Polity*, v § 42

WIPF & STOCK · Eugene, Oregon

Wipf and Stock Publishers
199 W 8th Ave, Suite 3
Eugene, OR 97401

Athanasius
His Life and Life Work
By Reynolds, Henry Robert
Softcover ISBN-13: 978-1-6667-3343-3
Hardcover ISBN-13: 978-1-6667-2808-8
eBook ISBN-13: 978-1-6667-2809-5
Publication date 8/4/2021
Previously published by
The Religious Tract Society, 1889

This edition is a scanned facsimile of
the original edition published in 1889.

PREFACE.

THE life-story of Athanasius has often been told During half a century the biography of this man becomes a history of Christianity and of the Church, when both were alike face to face with a Pagan reaction The extant writings of Athanasius—which have been edited and also translated in convenient form for the English reader—cast a bright light upon contemporary religious politics and parties, proclaim the dawn of rational exegesis, and are especially valuable from the eagerness with which the author dealt with ideas and things rather than with terms or phrases The ecclesiastical histories of Eusebius, Rufinus, Socrates, Sozomen, Theodoret and Evagrius, as well as the fragments of the Arian Philostorgius, when these are checked by Athanasius himself, warmed by the studied panegyrics of Gregory of Nazianzus, criticised in the light of the epistles of Julian and the pages of the Roman historians or Greek sophists, furnish abundant material for the student of the fourth century

All the modern historians of the century have used these materials with varying success Gibbon himself leads the way, and almost forgets to sneer in face of the Patriarch of Alexandria Neander, in his *General History of the Church*, and in his monograph on Julian , Dr. Newman, in his *History of the Arians*, and Bishop Kaye, in his *Council of Nicæa*, Dr Hort, in *Two Dissertations*, and Dr. Gwatkin, *Studies in Arianism*, and Dr Dorner on *the History of Doctrine of the Person of Christ*, (Div. 1 , vol. 2, E.T) have discussed the opinions of Athanasius with consummate ability. The Lives of Athanasius by Cave, Tillemont, Mohler and Fialon , the monographs by Dean Stanley in his *Lectures on the Eastern Church*, the histories of Dr. Neale, Albert de Broglie, and Villemain , Canon Bright's introduction to his edition of the *Four Discourses*, and Dr Newman's notes to the translation of the discourses and tracts, are all charged with information.

While these pages have been in the printer's hands, Archdeacon Farrar's *Lives of the Fathers* have appeared, and the story of the 'Life' is presented anew in brilliant and most effective form. Every fresh student must select the portions of this vast theme which seem to him to provide matters for deepest reflection. I have endeavoured to

PREFACE.

tell the story of his life very simply, from the standpoint of the religious consciousness rather than that of political, ecclesiastical or national reconstruction. The career of Athanasius carries the reader from Alexandria to Rome, from the episcopal throne to the profoundest recesses of the wilderness, shows him to be the living martyr in a great variety of circumstances, but in them all the heart of Athanasius burns and throbs with the impulse of one stupendous thought.

In the second and third centuries many controversies on the subject of the Godhead and the incarnation had been current, but for the most part believers encountered little difficulty in combining a belief in the oneness of the Godhead with their reverence for the Lord Jesus. They had suffered more trouble from Docetism, and from virtual denial of His *humanity*, than from any doubt about His Divinity. But in the fourth century many burning questions arose which demanded settlement. If Jesus be true Man, how can we worship Him? Have we accidentally slipped back into the Pagan worship of the demi-god, or are we trembling on the verge of Pantheism? What is the nature of this Divinity that we attribute to the Christ? Is the Divine glory which we ascribe to our Lord that of a deified man, or that of the incarnate Father, or does it proceed from the full union of the Son of God with man? Who is this Son of God?

The Christian Church was compelled to answer these questions, or die. Criticism is always being forced upon believers. Notwithstanding all the defects of ecclesiastics, the passions of princes, the ambition of courtiers and prelates, the arrogance of philosophers, yet the Christian consciousness of the fourth century, led by the Spirit of truth, came to the conclusion that it must, could, and would cling as for dear life to the unity of God, to the real humanity of Jesus, and to the eternal essential Divinity of the Christ, that no element of this sublime trilogy could be, or need be, sacrificed.

If this result—as important to the nineteenth century as it was to the fourth—was achieved by the sanctified intelligence of that age, it may be gathered from the record before us that, under God, the Church at large owes this victory to the life and life-work of Athanasius of Alexandria.

CONTENTS.

CHAPTER I.

	PAGE
THE SCENE AND CONDITIONS OF A VITAL CONTROVERSY	9
(1) Alexandria	9
(2) The Church at Alexandria and the Civil Power.	14
(3) The Conditions of Theological Controversy	16

CHAPTER II.

THE EARLY DAYS OF ATHANASIUS 21

CHAPTER III

ARIUS AND THE COUNCIL OF NICÆA . . . 25

CHAPTER IV

THE MELETIAN SCHISM 38

CHAPTER V.

ATHANASIUS, ARCHBISHOP OF ALEXANDRIA . . . 39

CHAPTER VI

ATHANASIUS IN EXILE AT TRÈVES (TRIER), AND WHAT HAPPENED IN THE INTERIM	52
(1) The Dedication of the Church of the Holy Sepulchre and the Resurrection	56
(2) The Eusebian Synod at Constantinople, and the Condemnation of Marcellus	57
(3) The Death of Arius	59
(4) The Death of Constantine the Great . .	60

CHAPTER VII.

THE RETURN OF ATHANASIUS FROM HIS FIRST EXILE AND THE COMMENCEMENT OF THE SECOND EXILE 62

CHAPTER VIII.

THE COUNCIL OF SARDICA AND THE SECOND RETURN OF ATHANASIUS   70

CHAPTER IX.

THE RESUMPTION OF THE ARIAN PERSECUTION, AND THE THIRD EXILE 74

CHAPTER X.

THE MINISTRY OF THE WILDERNESS 90
    (1) The Fate of the Church in Egypt 92
    (2) The Writings of Athanasius during this Exile . 95
    (3) The Four Discourses against the Arians . . 99
    (4) The Divisions in the Arian Party . . 116
    (5) The Divinity of the Holy Spirit . . . 127

CHAPTER XI.

THE ACCESSION OF JULIAN, AND THE THIRD RESTORATION OF ATHANASIUS TO HIS SEE . . . 129

CHAPTER XII

THE ACTS OF ATHANASIUS ON HIS REAPPEARANCE AFTER HIS SIX YEARS OF EXILE 139

CHAPTER XIII

THE CAUSE AND ISSUE OF THE FOURTH EXILE OF ATHANASIUS   153

CHAPTER XIV.

THE FIFTH EXILE AND CLOSING YEARS OF ATHANASIUS . . 164

CHAPTER XV.

THE CHARACTER OF ATHANASIUS 180

ATHÁNASIUS.

CHAPTER I.

THE SCENE AND CONDITIONS OF A VITAL CONTROVERSY.

(1) *Alexandria.*

BEFORE proceeding to tell the story of Athanasius, I desire to bring to the reader's recollection a few facts concerning the celebrated city where the youth and early manhood of the illustrious Bishop were passed, where he won his greatest victories, and where he suffered his most grievous humiliations, from the archiepiscopal throne of which he was frequently driven into ignominious exile, to which he was again and again restored amid enthusiasm which transcended the triumph of a Roman Cæsar, where he contended with the enemies of his faith and Church, and where at length, after a nominal occupancy of the see for forty-seven years, he was allowed to die in peace.

Compared with other cities of Egypt, Alexandria had few associations with the venerable past. Memphis, On, Saïs, Thebes, and Abydos gloried in records dating back through millenniums of royal dynasties, and were enriched by palaces, pyramids, tombs, libraries, museums and universities hoary with age before the first effort was made to utilize the splendid

site of what became the third if not the second city of
the Roman world.

Recent discoveries have proved that Greek thought
and language, Greek merchandise and military craft,
had, at the town of Naucratis, a few miles to the west
of Alexandria, already obtained a sure foothold long
before the approach of Alexander of Macedon. Silent
influences had been at work which made the bloodless
victory of Alexander possible. That gifted but inflated
hero cannot be credited with prophetic insight or any
prevision of the extraordinary fortune of the city the
outline of which he planned in the year 320 B C. He
found that there was the possibility of safe harbour-
age for his triremes; he shrewdly conjectured that it
might be made into a useful mercantile port and a
granary of first-class importance for his Ægean cities.
A Greek city might, as he thought, prove a position
from which he could dominate the turbulent population
of the valley of the Nile. Alexandria owes its cele-
brity less to its founder than to the skill, splendour and
ingenuity of his successors, and to their love of literature, science and archæology. A demonstrative ability
of no mean order was displayed by the Ptolemaic
princes, the descendants of Alexander's general, Lagos,
upon whom this sumptuous appanage of the Mace-
donian victories descended.

Alexander himself selected the site, a six-mile strip
of sandy soil between the Lake Mareotis and the sea.
The Ptolemies built the walls, and also the mole (*hep-
tastadium*) between the island of Pharos and the main-
land, and erected the vast street of palaces, nearly six
miles in length, extending from the Canopic to the
desert gate, faced with colonnades and enriched by
temples for the worship of the Egyptian Serapis and
Ptah, as well as of Poseidon and other Hellenic deities.

Alexander never saw the completion of his own design, although one of these buildings was the mausoleum where his body lay for a century in a coffin of gold.

The Ptolemies encouraged an immigration to Alexandria of Jews, who formed at one time a third of the entire population. They resided in the north-eastern extremity of the city, with a temple and with jurisdiction and an 'Ethnarch' or 'Alabarch' of their own. The Greek population came next in order, and the Egyptian quarter formed the west wing of the city. Beyond the walls on the west was the extensive Necropolis, the catacombs and memorials of which still stretch away into the desert.

The Lake Mareotis on the south received and was sweetened by the waters of the Nile, being fed by canals, which also carried through the city the same waters, and were delivered at last into the royal port, on the west of the great mole.

The sea-line on both sides of the mole was furnished by quays and dockyards of great extent and admirable arrangement; while at the eastern end of the lengthened line were the huge granaries, the stores of which, replenished by the fertile Nile, were often the resort of famine-stricken provinces, and were jealously watched and financed by the imperial authority.

The long, narrow island called Pharos protected the two harbours from the northern winds. This was a limestone rock of dazzling whiteness, and upon it the celebrated lighthouse was erected by Ptolemy Soter and his successor. It rose 400 feet in height, and must have been a conspicuous landmark, just as its diminished successor is at the present day.

The central Greek quarter was dignified by the great museum, library, and lecture-rooms. This magnificent group of buildings, adorned by obelisks and surrounded by colonnades of costly marbles, was connected with the royal palace, which stood on the projecting neck of land called Lochias. The library, partly deposited here, and partly housed in the Serapeium, was of prodigious extent, containing from four to seven hundred thousand volumes. Here, among others, were the collections of the Kings of Pergamos; and though in the blockade of the city by Julius Cæsar great damage was done to it, and still more in the reign of Theodosius, when the anti-pagan iconoclasm reached its highest enthusiasm, the library was not finally wrecked until the brutal orders of the Khalif Omar decreed its destruction 640 A.D.

Here were authentic and invaluable copies of the plays of Æschylus, Sophocles, and Euripides. Here were the stores of learning brought from Heliopolis (the On of Scripture) and from the Ramesseium of Thebes. Here, doubtless, were the original and most costly copies of the Greek translation of the Old Testament, here the sources from which Clemens Alexandrinus drew the substance of his *Stromata*—the materials which aided Origen in the compilation of his Hexapla, and unique MSS., which would have thrown a blaze of light upon the religious history of Egypt, Assyria, and Palestine, if they had not fallen a prey to civil broils, ecclesiastical animosities, and Moslem fanaticism. Here Euclid expounded the principles of mathematics, and Aratus and Callimachus the laws of poetry; here the great commentators on Aristotle flourished; and the Neoplatonists—Aristobulus, Philo, Ammonius Saccas—established their chief schools of thought. Here the Gnostic leaders endeavoured to unriddle the mystery of the Universe, and were brought into violent contact with the learned Jews and the philosophic teachers of Christianity.

The president of the Museum was one of the four chief magistrates of the city.

The Egyptian quarter lay still farther to the west, on the site of the small town of Rhacotis, and was dignified by the celebrated Serapeium, devoted to the honours and mysteries of the worship of Osiris-Apis, a probable blending of Nature-worship as imaged in the sun-god with the highest form of animal life. The population, amounting in the time of Christ to half a million, was probably little less in the days of Constantine, Constantius, Julian and Valens. Though Christianity had made a stronghold for itself, and had brought into its fold Jews and Greeks, Egyptians and Asiatics, abolishing or minimizing their fundamental antagonism, yet the strong tendencies of the separate nationalities would still assert themselves.

Other cities, like Antioch and Ephesus, Tarsus, Cæsarea, and Corinth, were filled with denizens of many lands; yet there was no one site where so many intellectual forces were blended; where such profoundly diverse elements stood face to face; where merchandise and letters, hoary tradition and agile scepticism, the grim forms of animal worship and the delicate beauty of Greek art, confronted each other so directly; where superstition was more besotted or speculation more acute; where the claims of a concrete theocracy were more pitilessly handled by a critical philosophy, one which reduced all supposed revelations and history to mere thought-forms; where literature and science seemed to give an equal joy, where, at the same time, games and all species of sensuous amusements were frowned upon by anchorets, who made their haunts in the caverns and creeks of the Pharos. The therapeutic and other cœnobites pursued their celibate life almost within hearing of the hum of the hippodrome, and within sight of the splendour and fashion of the royal street.

In the midst of this many-sided community stood also the catechetical school, where Pantænus, Clemens, and Origen discoursed on literature and metaphysics. Here also the Christian churches, which dated from the first century and from the evangelistic labours of St. Mark, stood face to face with all these contentious elements and mutually destructive forces, and were easily tempted to an eclectic combination of ideas and to some laxity of ecclesiastical discipline.

(2) *The Church at Alexandria and the Civil Power.*

At certain epochs in the history of the Church the persecuting edicts of the Roman emperors fell with malign fury upon the Christians of Alexandria. The annals of the community were early stained with the blood of martyrs. In the reign of Septimius Severus, at the commencement of the third century, the new edicts which were issued against secret societies, and which repressed all proselytism, bore with special cruelty on the Jews of Alexandria and on the Christians of Northern Africa. Clemens Alexandrinus wrote: 'Many are daily crucified, beheaded, burned before our very eyes.' Leonidas, the father of the youthful Origen, was beheaded for his open confession of the faith, and was encouraged to persevere to the end by the enthusiastic persuasions of his son.

Potomiæna, a virgin of rare beauty, after being threatened with atrocious dishonour, was preserved from this fearful indignity only to be slowly consumed in boiling pitch. But a period of rest occurred during the ignoble reigns of Caracalla and Elagabalus, and under the tolerant *régime* of Alex. Severus. His murderer and successor, Maximinus Thrax, raged furiously for a brief period against the Christians; but the Gordians and Philip, from 238-249 A.D., did not press the execution of the unrepealed edicts, while a tradition arose that Philip personally desired to be admitted into the Christian Church.[1]

Cruel persecutions broke out in the reign of Decius Trajan, between 248-253 A.D., and during the episcopate of Dionysius the Church of North Africa suffered cruelly. Many, under fierce trial, apostatized, and their subsequent treatment provoked angry controversy in the Church. There were those who would show no mercy to men who had denied their Lord in the hour of darkness. There were others who urged a more lenient discipline, and suffered the traitors and apostates, on due repentance, to return to the fellowship of the Church. The number who fell shows the barbarity of the persecution. Fabianus, Bishop of Rome, Alexander of Jerusalem, Babylas of Antioch, were faithful unto death. Origen suffered imprisonment and torture.

It is unnecessary here to touch, even in the slightest way, the persecutions under Valerian; nor can we pause to contemplate the gleam of light and imperial favour which broke over the persecuted Church during the reign of Gallienus, when Christianity became a *religio licita,* and the churches in various parts of the empire held land and property by legal right. Twenty years of external peace sufficed to introduce Christians into high places of trust and honour, and to bring the exclusive claims of Christ more thoroughly face to face with the gorgeous but undermined paganism of the empire. The truth dawned upon the fanatical

[1] Though this fact is asserted by Dionysius of Alex. (Eus, *H.E*, vii 10), yet there is no trace on Philip's coins, nor any recorded fact in his history, calculated to confirm it, while the silence of Origen throws the gravest doubt on the statement.

and savage pagan Galerius, whom Diocletian had first
entrusted with the Cæsarship and afterwards constituted a fellow Augustus, that Christianity was a rival
even to his military autocracy. The first notes of
alarm were sounded in the year 298; these sent a
thrill of apprehension through the widely scattered
community, from Britain and Gaul to the southern
confines of Egypt, from Carthage to Edessa. From
that first act of Galerius till the overthrow of Licinius
and the sole principate of Constantine, the tocsin of
war never ceased, and the Church passed through a
Red Sea of blood to its Promised Land.

Eusebius (*H. E*, viii) enlarges with warning words
upon the unmentionable horrors of the persecution in
the valley of the Nile. 'Men, women, and children
innumerable, steadfastly professing their faith and
trust in the Saviour, endured the scourge, the rack,
the pincers, and every other torture,—were burned,
drowned, beheaded, famished, crucified. . . .
Scarcely a day passed for several years but a number
of Christians were tortured and destroyed, and as soon
as one company had received their sentence another
crowded up to the tribunal to declare themselves.
. . . In the agonies of death they sang psalms and
songs of praise to their blessed Creator, to which I
myself was eye-witness.'

Alexandria was the scene of numberless martyrdoms,
and the Bishop Peter, with Faustus, Dius, and Ammonius, his presbyters,—also Hesychius, Pachomius,
Theodorus, bishops of other Egyptian churches, fell
victims to this terrible scourge (Eus , *H. E*, viii. 13).

(3) *The Conditions of Theological Controversy.*

During a whole generation, from Maximinus to
Diocletian, virtual tranquillity prevailed, and the

A VITAL CONTROVERSY.

Church at Alexandria developed its internal resources, and occupied itself with grave discussions on some of the profoundest mysteries of the Divine existence and of its relation to the universe. The great controversy which broke over the Church of the third century has survived even to the present day; and it throws important illumination on the more conspicuous strife which embittered the long episcopate of Athanasius. A few words on this subject will facilitate the understanding of the later controversies.

Many events conspired during the third century to emphasize the grand Hebrew tradition concerning the unity of the Godhead. This great inheritance of the fathers had, in previous ages, been grossly imperilled by fierce temptations to succumb to the Nature-worship and idolatry of the nations which by turns trampled upon the sacred people. They fell into the snare, and suffered the consequences of disloyalty to their supreme inheritance. At length the burning words of their prophets and the fiery trials of massacre, exile and bondage consumed their evil propensities in these directions, and they had emerged from the crucible convinced, dogmatic, fervent in their unalterable assent to the most central truth of their entire system: 'Hear, O Israel, Jehovah, thy Lord, is One.' Though there were many that were called gods and lords, yet to them there was no god but *One*. Idolatry in all its forms was the unspeakable abomination.

When at length the restored nation fell, and the holy city once more became a desolation, this proud conviction animated their scattered settlements. In Asia Minor, in Cyprus and Cyrene, in Rome and Alexandria, whatever else the most bigoted Jew was compelled to surrender, he maintained with passionate eagerness his belief in the unity of God. We rejoice

in the discovery, which is becoming better understood
day by day, that the profoundest minds in Egypt, in
Persia and Greece, had grasped the underlying unity
of the Divine Being, and regarded the prevailing
polytheism as doomed to perish. The philosophical
Jews, who came to some extent under the influence of
Greek culture, were peculiarly sensitive to the peril of
using any phrases which tended to anthropomorphize
this sublime spiritual unity, or even to speak of the
one God as doing, being or saying aught which could
be construed into a division of His essence. The
separation between the infinite and eternal One, and
either His finite creation or His mortal worshippers,
became more and more oppressive.

It is true that Philo, the Jew of Alexandria, had
found a method of interpretation which sought to
accommodate the statements of the Scriptures to the
forms of Platonic thought; and, in order to save at
once the absolute uniqueness of God and the supposed
contact of the Divine essence with man, attributed to
the Logos (Word) of God, to the Divine reason, to the
sum of Divine ideas, all that was spoken of in the
Pentateuch as the communion of Jehovah with men.
God Himself retired into the inaccessible depth of
absolute Being.

Now Christians held, without attempting any
solution of the difficulties that presented themselves,
not only the unity of God, but the Divine nature and
prerogatives of the Son of God. They passionately
loved the Man Christ Jesus. They would not swerve
from the position that He had at least a human
mother—that He lived as a man, taught, suffered,
hungered, loved, and at last died upon the cross.
Often sorely tempted to believe that His human condition was a phantom, and His seeming manhood an

unreality, yet neither Gnostic Ebionitism nor the ingenious speculation of Marcion or Cerinthus shook the faith of the infant Church in the genuine humanity of Christ. Nevertheless they held that He had an existence before His birth into this world, and that the Divine element, force and authority in Him lifted His whole personality above all other men. He was more than Moses or Aaron, greater than Solomon, more prophetic than Elias, more priestly than Melchizedec, and stood to the whole human race in a light which answered even to the Adam. He was Head, Archetype, Master, Judge, Lord of all men. They offered Him divine homage, worshipped Him as God, trusted to His infinite sympathy and His saving might, went willingly to the cross or to the fire or the amphitheatre rather than revile Him or place the majesty of the *Divus Cæsar* on a par with His.

Nor was it the Eternal Father who (they believed) had been incarnated in Him, but the *Son* of God, 'the brightness of the Father's glory,' the image of the invisible essence, 'the Word of God,' the only begotten of the Father, who had thus taken human nature up into Himself. In thus speaking of the Father and the Son of the Father, they went perilously near to a virtual repudiation of the unity of God. So that while simple minds easily and without any consciousness of contradiction held that God was one, and yet that Christ was Son of God, thoughtful men resolved if possible to justify the seeming paradox, and proposed different methods of doing it.

Without touching upon his numerous antecedents and predecessors in the task, special attention is called to Sabellius of Ptolemais, in Northern Africa, who maintained that the *Unity* of the Godhead was a more fundamental truth than the *Divinity* of the Son of

God, and endeavoured to apply the pantheistic solution to the problem. He urged that the Eternal Father was the silent, inactive, all but impersonal Essence, the *Monad*; but when He uttered Himself, He became *Dyad*. The Word was the principle of the creation, the Spirit of God was only the activity of this creative energy in man. The Father, Son and Spirit (said he) are not in any sense individuals, but only aspects, appearances, of one indivisible Essence. So far as human history is concerned, these appearances and manifestations had (he thought) taken different phases. The Father revealed Himself under the Old Covenant; the Lord Jesus Christ was, as Son of God, another phase of the same Divinity; the Holy Spirit manifested the same Essence in the life of the Church. These were reabsorbed into the eternal Essence when they had accomplished their work, and were strictly finite in all that characterized them.

Views akin to those of Sabellius had long troubled the Church; but when set forth with eloquence and enthusiasm and by appeal to logic and Scripture, they called for the protest of the Alexandrine Church. Dionysius of Alexandria, and afterwards Origen, called the mind of the Church to two great defects in the speculation. Dionysius condemned the transitory character thus attributed to Christ, and the temporary value of the whole manifestation. Jesus Christ was to him, 'the same yesterday, to-day, and for ever;' and the relation therefore of the Son to the Father was a reality and not a philosophic dream. He went so far in this direction as to use language which could be subsequently quoted to show that his views scarcely differed from those of Arius. Origen, perhaps, exposed himself to a similar charge, but he further exhibited another grievous defect in the position of Sabellius—

he urged, that it sacrificed the true humanity of Jesus Christ, and abolished that union of the Divine and human in Him which was virtually involved in every prayer and sacrament of the martyr Church.

Dionysius of Rome criticised the expressions of his brother and namesake of Alexandria, and showed him that if he held the *creation* of the Son by the Father, then there was an eternity during which the Father existed as the solitary Monad, without the Son and object of His love. Origen boldly breasted the amazing difficulty that thus offered itself by the declaration of the eternal generation of the Son; in other words, by the speculation that the relation between the Son and the Father was eternal—was fundamental to the very essence of God—that from eternity to eternity, before all worlds, now and for evermore, this flowing from the eternal fountain of Being must have been proceeding. The Son was begotten in the eternal Now. Apart from the echoes and consequences of this supposed solution of the mystery, the Arian controversy, which occupied the whole active life of Athanasius, is unintelligible.

CHAPTER II.

THE EARLY DAYS OF ATHANASIUS.

ATHANASIUS was born in 297 A.D.; and though he could not remember the violent outbreak of persecution under Maximian in 303, yet he must have been eye and ear witness of the loathsome proceedings and inhuman cruelties of Maximin Daza in 311. Upon his young spirit must have been branded the ineffaceable memorial of these deeds. The heroism of holy women, saintly bishops, and youthful confessors of the faith, doubtless inspired some of that indomitable endurance, that courageous loyalty to conviction, that consuming zeal for the glory of Christ, which characterized his entire career.

In 313, when Athanasius was sixteen years of age, Alexander was consecrated to the episcopate of Alexandria in place of the martyred Peter. This simple chronological fact does much to dissipate the interesting story first told by Rufinus, and copied from Rufinus by Socrates (*H. E.*, 1. 15), and by Sozomen (*H. E.*, 11. 17). It runs thus: that the venerable bishop was in the company of his presbyters looking from the window of his house upon the sea-shore, and there espied children at play. Their amusement consisted in one of their number, apparently with due solemnity, baptizing his companions. They were brought before the bishop, and confessed their act. Bishop Alexander, finding that the ritual of the Church had been complied with, admitted, so it is said, the validity of the ordinance in this case, and shortly afterwards arranged that the 'boy bishop,'—no other than Athanasius,—should become his private secretary. All that the story is good for is a testimony to the precocity of the youth, and his education probably under the sanction and direction of the ecclesiastics of Alexandria.

Many influences must have conspired to mould the character and direct the thought of Athanasius. He saw heathen worship in its most gorgeous form and august ceremonial. Philosophy was grappling with some of the difficult questions which find their only solution in revealed religion. Moreover the illustrious Christian teachers proved that they were familiar with

THE EARLY DAYS OF ATHANASIUS. 23

all that either science or philosophy, scepticism or magical device, had to offer, with all speculative hypotheses touching the origin of the universe, and all Gnostic dreams about the development of man. Before the outbreak of the Arian heresy the mind of the young student began not only to ponder the questions and answers which had been heard in the catechetical school, but to produce apologetic and doctrinal treatises of his own. He wrote when not more than twenty-one years of age his works entitled, *Against the Gentiles*, and *Concerning the Incarnation*. In his early manhood he compared the gods of the nations, their mythical deeds, their insufficient and their corrupting travesties of the Divine idea, with the teaching of Scripture, with the character of Christ, and with the Divinity of the Crucified.[1]

We see in his work on *The Incarnation* a youthful mind untrammelled by controversies of later years. His object was to show a reason for the incarnation in the eternal purpose of redemption. He did not hesitate to use language then which he would subsequently have shunned. He laid great emphasis on ' the *body* ' which the Word assumed, and he also is apparently persuaded that 'corruption itself in death no longer has force against men by virtue of the Word dwelling in them through His one body.' Since 'men can learn from men about divine things,' the incarnation made the knowledge of God possible. The ultimate ground of the incarnation and redeeming death of the Word was the goodness and lovingkindness of God. There is scarcely any treatise of Athanasius which surpasses this for the splendour of its diction. Per-

[1] The second of these treatises has been recently translated in the 'Christian Classics' series of the Religious Tract Society, by Mr. Herbert Bindley, of Merton College, Oxford.

haps the suspicion of juvenility is suggested by the
daring speculation and brilliant phrase; but there is
a modern tone about the argument which startles
the reader. The death-blow dealt to idolatry by the
incarnation is grandly conceived, and the whole Church
of Alexandria must have felt that a new and notable
power had risen up in its midst.

Athanasius was acquainted with Homer and with
his interpreters, with Plato and his disciples, and with
the later and wilder forms of the Neoplatonic philosophy. He learned in the schools how to quote these
Greek poets and sages, who maintained the reality of
the Divine Presence in the world, and who personally
yearned after life beyond the grave.

Modern research has thrown the gravest doubt over
the supposition that Athanasius was the author of *The
Life of Anthony*, and consequently over the romantic
story of the connection between the greatest ascetic
and the most illustrious theologian of the fourth
century. It is not probable that Athanasius ever
communed with Anthony, or 'poured water on his
hands,' or was initiated by the mighty monk into the
life of the monastery, or wrote his life; yet his subsequent career proved that he had learned the secret of
self-restraint, the special calling of the celibate, the
honours and privileges of the religious life. Still, we
cannot attribute to him the fulsome praise of virginity
so conspicuous in the writings of Tertullian and
Cyprian, of Jerome and Basil.

Athanasius was profoundly impressed in these his
earliest days with the transcendent significance of the
person of the Son of God incarnate. He saw every
other truth in the light of the knowledge of the glory
of God in the face of Christ, and all the history of
man and revelation appeared to revolve around this

sublime centre; consequently he was helpful to his friend and father, Alexander, the Archbishop or Patriarch (*Papa*) of Alexandria, when Arius first broke in upon the scene. Then it happened that he was elevated from the position of secretary to that of deacon of the Church, or, as some writers say, 'archdeacon,' of the metropolitan diocese.

CHAPTER III.

ARIUS AND THE COUNCIL OF NICÆA.

ARIUS was no novice. He was forty years older than Athanasius, had been entrusted with the care of a church at Baucalis, had given umbrage to Peter, the martyr bishop, and had even been excommunicated for defending the cause of Meletius. He was a man of gigantic stature, but his limbs seemed loosely hung together; gaunt in feature, yet with a bewitching, captivating manner, which gave him exceptional influence over the women of his charge. He was, however, ascetic in habit and blameless in life. Like Eusebius of Nicomedia, he had been a pupil of Lucian at Antioch, and had learned the art of a narrow, hairsplitting logic. He could drive his human analogies recklessly into the doctrine of the Godhead.

Lucid definition, finality of form, purged of all mystery, seemed essential to him, and he was careless about the issues of his clean-cutting syllogisms. He was ambitious and eager, and believed that he was not only Scriptural and right in his ideas, but that Alexander was in grievous error and deadly sin. He thought that he himself and those who believed as he did were alone orthodox and Christian.

More than that, he spoke of the party of Alexander as heretics, and of the views of some of them as an 'impiety to which we could not listen, though we were threatened by them with a thousand deaths' (Theod., *H. E.*, i. 5).

But he was confronted at Alexandria with a courage, an acuteness, and a logic quite equal to his own, with this additional peculiarity—that his antagonist saw what he did not—the deadly issues of his negations. The lean, gaunt man, with his vehement gestures, strange contortions—perhaps the result of physical pain—with his large following among ascetics and holy women and other ladies and laics, maintained the position that the Divinity of Christ, that the Divine element in the Christ, that 'the Son of God,' could in no sense be regarded as of the same substance with the Father. Arius urged that if He were a Son, there was a moment in the past eternity when, though before all worlds, He was generated and created by the *will* of the Father. 'There was when He was not.' 'He was not before He was begotten.'

Many of these speculations had their rise in the Neoplatonic schools of Alexandria, where it was held that a certain divinity accrued to the three elements of the metaphysic *triad* : 'the Good,' the 'Logos,' the 'Soul' of the universe. They had exaggerated and stretched the old distinctions or hypostases current in the earlier Platonic schools, until they had made the third hypostasis identical with 'the soul of the world,' and a veritable creature. The views of Arius as to the Divinity of the Son rapidly degenerated into such an estimate of the incarnate Son as to regard Him as mere man, and closely to approach that later speculation. But Arius vehemently opposed Sabellianism, and in his reaction from that pantheistic tendency came to the perilous position that the Son of God was a created Being, a derived God, a second God, and, as it was at once perceived, a 'demi-god,' allied to 'the gods many and lords many' who had just been driven out of the mind and heart of Christendom. He did not refuse to worship Christ; but in this he only further excited the indignation of the Alexandrines. The great teachers of the Church held that the worship of any being less than, or different from, the only God was idolatry, and involved the re-entrance of paganism into Christian theology.

Great effort was made by Arius to diffuse his views, not only among the occupants of the chief sees of Eastern Christendom, but among all classes of the population. By his ascetic regimen and his strange manners, by his emaciated appearance, his uncouth attire and versatile gifts, by his rude crop of unkempt hair, by his agitated voice and shaking limbs, he exerted a weird influence over the population of Alexandria, as afterwards over that of Constantinople.

It is difficult to form a sound idea of his character; for in pursuance of his aims he gravely compromised his position by shocking the Christian sentiment of his contemporaries. He produced a poetical or rhythmical jingle of verses called *Thalia,* of which Athanasius preserves two considerable specimens (in his *First Discourse against the Arians,* § 5, and in his treatise *Concerning the Synods of Ariminium and Seleucia,* § 15), the demerit of which was the metre adopted rather than the terms actually employed to familiarize the popular mind with the points of the controversy. The effect was comparable to that produced by Butler's poem of *Hudibras,* or as if now the doctrine of the atonement were ridiculed by being described contemptuously in the lilting lines of *Tam o' Shanter.*

The Greek metre called *Sotadean* had been used for drinking-songs and lascivious dance-music, and when used to describe the mysteries of the Divine nature had a blasphemous effect upon reverential minds. Part of the consequence was that the lower orders as well as the partizans of the court or the clergy were entirely preoccupied with superficial aspects of the great controversy.

Gregory of Nyssa thus indicated the result on the popular mind: 'Men of yesterday, mere mechanics, off-hand dogmatists in theology, servants too and slaves that have been flogged, runaways from servile work, are solemn with us and philosophical about things incomprehensible. With such the whole city is full,— its smaller gates, forums, squares, thoroughfares; the clothes vendors, the money lenders, the victuallers. Ask about pence, and he will discuss the Generate and the Ingenerate; inquire the price of bread, he answers, "Greater is the Father, and the Son is subject"; say that a bath would suit you, and he defines that the Son is out of nothing.'[1]

By one means or other Arius won over to his views, and was able to secure the co-operation of, no less a a man than Eusebius of Nicomedia, the favoured prelate of the court. The vigorous letters written in reply to Arius by Alexander of Alexandria to his namesake at Constantinople and to many other bishops, are strongly suspected to have been the work of the young secretary and deacon, Athanasius.

This is not the place to detail the steps by which Arius was at length summoned before a synod of one hundred bishops at Alexandria, in the year 321, and formally excommunicated; nor how Constantine, who

---

[1] *Orat. de Deitate Filii*, iii. 466 ; Neander, *C. H.*, iv. 61.

had heard of the controversy, thought that he could settle it by an imperial mandate, in which he counselled Alexander and Arius immediately to come to terms, and not to contend about mere words. We cannot here enumerate the various steps which preceded the summoning of the Œcumenical (or worldwide) Council of Nicæa, the first of those imposing parliaments of bishops which were supposed to represent the entire Church, and to be gifted with heavenly wisdom. The assembly was graced by the presence of the Emperor himself.

Eusebius leaves it doubtful (*Vita Const.*, iii. 6) whether the stately entrance of Constantine into the assembly, in his robes of imperial purple and diadem of gold, took place on the first or last day of the council. His modesty in the presence of this assembly of the notables was displayed by his refusal to sit down until his 'dearest friends' beckoned to him to do so. He made an oration to them in Latin, which was interpreted into the Greek language. It was surcharged with a grave desire for peace and harmony and unanimity of faith; and when the angrier spirits among them sought to place their petitions and counter-petitions before him, he refused to read them, but caused them to be burnt before their eyes in a brazier.

The assembly was graced by delegates from the Bishop of Rome, by Hosius of Cordova, by the two Alexanders, by the two Eusebii, by bishops who had been blinded and mutilated in the terrible persecutions under Decius and Maximian, and by about seventeen bishops who openly sympathized with Arius; three hundred and eighteen in all. A crowd of ecclesiastics, monks, presbyters and deacons were present in the city, in attendance upon their bishops. There were many questions to resolve and canons to pass with reference to the Meletian schism, the precedence and consecration of ecclesiastics, and the mode of determining the Easter festival. Eusebius represents this particular question as the most important of all; but the chief debate, the one all-absorbing theme, was the Divinity of the Son of God. No one repudiated the Divine nature of the Son, yet it soon became evident that everything was at stake in the meaning which was attributed to that sublime conception.

In fighting the battle, no single combatant became so conspicuous as the young deacon Athanasius, who was not, at that date, more than twenty-eight years of age. He was the life and soul, the intellectual athlete and leader of the great conflict. He was physically extremely unlike his notorious antagonist. Diminutive in form, yet with piercing eye, beautiful face 'as of an angel,' and of fascinating expression, agile and graceful in movement, active and resolute, and capable of boundless effort, he moved hither and thither, everywhere advising, expounding, enforcing the *pros* and *cons* of the mighty controversy. Hated by the friends of Arius, contributing to the triumphant condemnation of his views, Athanasius is mainly responsible for inserting one word in the *Symbolum Nicænum* which the Arians would not and dared not adopt. They admitted all the august phrases which declared that Christ was '*the only begotten Son of God, begotten of the Father before all worlds,*'—that He was '*very God of very God,*' laying emphasis on the '*of*'; they could accept the incarnation, suffering, death and resurrection of Christ; but by all their discourse and correspondence they utterly repudiated His absolute Divinity. He was not the eternal God, therefore He was a subordinate God. In the opinion of the great majority of the council, on such an hypothesis the Son of God could have been nothing different from a heathen demi-god.

Now there was a Sabellian watchword which unfortunately had been condemned in the previous century, when used by Paul of Samosata in the sense of physical, material identity, excluding all difference of personality between the Father and the Son. When, however, the assembled bishops felt more acutely than they could express the immense difference of view between themselves and the Arians, this word was suggested. The word was—HOMOOUSIOS, '*of one and the same substance (ousia) with the Father*'; it exactly conveyed what they meant, viz., that all the perfections and glories of the Father were by His begetting absolutely conveyed to the Son.

In the earlier clauses of the Creed, a phrase of similar import was introduced to define the expression 'begotten of the Father, only begotten, that is, from the substance of the Father.' This expression was afterwards omitted. Nevertheless, Athanasius, in his letter to the Emperor Jovian forty years later, when citing the Nicene Creed, leaves it intact. Athanasius informed the African bishops, a few years only before his death, of the scenes in the council which led to the insistence by the majority upon the terms which afterwards became so offensive to the Arian party. Theodoret (*H. E.*, i., c. 8) has preserved the passage. Athanasius, recalling the scene, said that the party of Eusebius was agreed with the rest in declaring that 'the Son is by nature the only begotten Son of God, the Word, the Power, and the Wisdom of the Father,' that He is 'very God of very God.' But the Eusebians took counsel, and decided that the Son of God was '*of* God,' just as all things were 'of

God,' no more, no less. To avoid this conclusion, says Athanasius, 'the bishops,' and by that he means the majority, wrote that He is 'of the substance of the Father.' The Arians (he adds), who were few in number, were again interrogated whether they would admit 'that the Son is not a creature, but the Power and the Wisdom and the Image of the Father; that He is eternal, in no respects differing from the Father, and that He is very God.' It was remarked that the Eusebians communicated with each other by signs, to the effect that these declarations were equally applicable to men—for it is said that *we* are the image and glory of God—quoting numerous Scriptures to that effect. The only way in which the Nicene Fathers could insist on the immeasurable dignity and glory of the Son of God was by using a term which prevented His Divinity from being degraded to the rank of creatureship.

Against the adoption of the term the sympathizers with Arius loudly protested. The obnoxious word became at once the symbol of the truth which was at stake, and it was used, not to abolish the fact of the generation or the personality of the Son, but to guard the absolute Deity of Christ, and yet maintain the veritable solity and unity of the Divine Being.

In addition to the formula thus enriched and decided, anathemas were recorded against those who adopted the Arian formulas, and therefore upon Arius himself.

The form of the Creed was an enlargement and modification of one that Eusebius, the Bishop of Cæsarea, had presented to the council as one that had been familiar to him from his childhood, as used in the churches of Jerusalem and Cæsarea, and satisfying, therefore, the demands of a less critical age. The whole of our subsequent narrative will be made more obvious if we present this document side by side with that which finally issued from the Council of Nicæa. The portions in which the two documents agree run across the line, and are in a separate type from the parts of the two documents in which they differ.

We believe in one God, the Father Almighty,

of the all things, | of all things,

visible and invisible, the Maker, and in one Lord Jesus Christ,

the Word of God. | the Son of God begotten of the Father, only begotten, that is, of the substance of the Father.

God of (ἐκ) God, Light of Light,

| very God of very God, begotten, not made, *being of one substance with* the Father.

Life of (ἐκ) Life, only begotten Son, the first brought forth of every creature, begotten of the Father before all ages. |

by whom the all things were made,

| both which are in heaven and which are on earth.

who

| for the sake of us men and

for our salvation
| came down;

was made flesh,

and had His own conversation among men ; | and became Man,

that He suffered and rose again the third day, and ascended

to the Father, and will come again in glory; | into the heavens, and is coming

to judge the living and dead.

We believe also in one Holy Spirit. | and in the Holy Spirit.

To the Nicene formula, as finally drafted, was also appended :

Those who say that 'there was when He was not,' and that 'He was not before He was begotten,' and that 'He was made of things that are not,' or who confess that the Son of God was of a different hypostasis or substance, or that He was created, or changeable, the Catholic and Apostolic Church anathematizes.

We will not here introduce the history of sundry modifications and additions, notably with reference to the Holy Spirit, which the document underwent. This is the form not only in which it occurs in Eusebius' letter to the church in Cæsarea, and in Athanasius' letter in 363 to the Emperor Jovian, but also the form in which it was quoted in later councils.

Thus the great council decided. Eventually, with certain exceptions, the assembled bishops signed the document. At first seventeen refused, among them Eusebius of Cæsarea and Eusebius of Nicomedia, Theognis of Nicæa, Secundus, Maris, and others. Ultimately, however, they all submitted, with the exception of Eusebius of Nicomedia, Theognis, Secundus, and Theonas. Into the time or occasion when they signed, and whether they simply refused to sign the anathemas against Arius himself, we do not enter. However this knotty point be finally settled, it is certain that Eusebius and Theognis were driven from their sees into exile for three years, and Arius was banished to Illyria.

Sozomen (ii. 21) explains the exile of Eusebius and Theognis as the punishment inflicted by Constantine upon them for their conduct in erasing their signatures from the Nicene formula, and in once more raising the discussions which he vainly thought he had permanently quelled. For a while Arianism seemed extinct; at least it was utterly humbled in the dust, and the *Homoousion* triumphed over the East as well as the West. Nevertheless the triumph was hardly celebrated when the reaction commenced, which acutely distracted the Church during half a century, and the effect of which has never been obliterated.

At length Eusebius and Arius were restored to the favour of Constantine, for they persuaded him that they, with the rest of their party, did substantially accept the Nicene doctrine and formula.

The vacillation of Constantine is a curious problem, and, in view of the vast interests at stake and the subsequent history of the struggle, it has almost a grotesque and cynical character. Constantine was accustomed to enforce and receive from his subordinates implicit military obedience. Harmony between the great ecclesiastical authorities in Africa, Asia Minor, Syria, and Italy was an imperial interest. He regarded the intensity of the contest with bewildered amazement, and could not understand that when once a form of faith had been drawn up there could be any further question. His mandate, his secular arm, ought to be sufficient to compel unity. Nothing but menacing and perilous audacity, and something approaching to the crime of treason, could account in his mind for the recusancy of the great leaders in this august debate.

The numerous letters of Constantine reveal a pathetic desire for agreement, and a not unnatural incapacity for grasping the gist of the controversy.

Modern writers, who have little or no sympathy with the position achieved at Nicæa, are disposed to minimize the importance of the conflict between those who were ready to admit the *resemblance* of the substance (*ousia*) of the Father to that of the Son, and those who urged the *sameness* of that substance. To crush the two ideas into two words, and to say that an *iota* (ι) alone represented the difference,[1] is to trifle with history. The angle of our modern vision may be very 'acute,' but if the two lines are projected into infinity, there is absolutely no limit to the arc which

---

[1] The great word *homoousios* (of one and the same substance) differs from *homoiousios* (of the like substance), in fact, in one letter only. But this one letter represents an immense and real difference. On neither side did any controversialist plead that the humanity of the Christ was uncreated, or other than the work of God's hands; but the discussion prevailed as to the increate character and essence of that Divine Personality which took human nature up into His own Being

will subtend the angle. The Divinity of Christ has to do with eternity; and unless He be 'the same yesterday, to-day, and for ever,' Christianity is an illusion to those who are seeking in it the salvation of the immortal soul of man.

It was the thing, however, and not the word, for which Athanasius contended, and for which he was prepared to suffer. In his numerous works he seldom used the technical term, and he admitted in his later years that it was capable of misconstruction; but the one point for which he was ready to sacrifice his life, and in the maintenance of which he shook the world, was the absolute unity of God, and the perfect Deity of the Son of God, who took human nature into Himself.

The circumstances were unique. No such crisis had ever occurred in the history of the Church. Doubtless, baptismal formulæ abounded. Short schedules of Christian doctrine and morality were in current use in different provinces of the empire, but never before had the leaders of the Church been called upon to formulate a creed. The step was novel and perilous, and was rendered all but imperative by the counter-formulas of those who wished to impress their ideas and enforce their hypothetical interpretations of Scripture upon their brethren. The use of phrases not found in Holy Scripture excited reasonable hostility. The very term *homoousios* excited jealousy and distrust among those who stood in the old paths and sensitively shrank from innovation, and the consequence was, that before the ink was dry which recorded the adhesion of the Eastern bishops to the Nicene formula, a powerful tendency had set in to abolish or reconsider it. This conservative reaction may do much to explain some of the strange scenes and melancholy conflicts which followed. It is lamentable that the victorious leaders of the *Homoousian* party at Nicæa were the first to set the miserable example of persecuting their theological opponents by using the weapons of exile and proscription which were subsequently wielded by the Arians against themselves.

CHAPTER IV.

THE MELETIAN SCHISM.

ONE further circumstance must be referred to before our narrative of the life of the deacon Athanasius can be safely proceeded with. During the episcopate of the martyr Peter, *i e*, between A.D. 300–311, the second important see in Egypt, that of Lycopolis (the modern *Siout*), was occupied by one Meletius (or Melitius), who, during an absence of Peter from his see, ventured without authority to consecrate bishops and ordain presbyters and to assume patriarchal functions. This was naturally resented by Peter. He called a synod of North African bishops, who deposed Meletius, and endeavoured to arrest these disorderly proceedings. Meletius was further charged with having escaped persecution by immoral concessions. This was never proved, nor was his personal orthodoxy ever impugned. The ecclesiastical difficulty was brought before the Council of Nicæa, which dealt leniently with the twenty-nine bishops who were in harmony with Meletius and with the presbyters and deacons ordained by him or them. The council decreed continuance of office to all, and nominal rank to Meletius himself, if bishops and clergy would recognise alike the primacy of the Bishop of Alexandria.

During the episcopate of Alexander, Meletius took no active part in maintaining a separate organization; but no sooner had Athanasius been invested with this dignity, and endeavoured to carry out the decision of the Council of Nicæa, than the bitterest feud arose between the adherents of the two Bishops of Lycopolis and Alexandria. The party of the former unfortunately identified themselves entirely with the violent reaction of Arianism and Eusebianism against the authority and position of Athanasius. To such an extent did this prevail that the very names, Meletian and Arian, became interchangeable, and the bitterest antagonism to the character and claims of Athanasius was fashioned and fostered by Meletian bishops. Meletius, on his death-bed, bequeathed his position as nominal Bishop of Lycopolis to his friend and follower, John Arcaph; nor did the schism thus originated disappear until the fifth century.

CHAPTER V.

ATHANASIUS, ARCHBISHOP OF ALEXANDRIA.

The venerable Alexander did not survive more than five months the excitement and agitations of the Council of Nicæa. Uncertainty prevails as to the exact date from which these months are to be reckoned. It is, however, probable that he lived until the spring of the year 326. On his death-bed he clearly and repeatedly called for Athanasius—then absent from Alexandria—and nominated him as his successor.

When the validity of the election and consecration was subsequently called in question, the Egyptian bishops issued an encyclical letter, publicly declaring that, with the consent of the laity of Alexandria and the enthusiasm of the people, they had consecrated Athanasius, a fact described by the bishop himself, and affirmed by Gregory of Nazianzus. One of the first mendacious charges of the Meletian and Arian party was that fifty-four bishops from Thebes and other parts of Egypt had met to fill the vacancy, but that seven of these bishops met, and, contrary to their oath, had clandestinely consecrated Athanasius (Soz., *H. E.*, ii. c. 17).

Meantime, Eusebius of Nicomedia and Theognis, by representing themselves as virtual signatories of the Creed of Nicæa, had secured revocation from their exile, and endeavoured to annul as far as possible the impression produced on the mind of Constantine by the decisions of the Œcumenical Council; and not only were they able to procure the recall of friends, but they were also eager to humiliate Athanasius by compelling him to admit the heresiarch to the communion of the Church. Eusebius, though sustained by the good-will of the Emperor, found that he had to deal with an unbending will, and with a man to whom the divine glory of the Christ was no mere question of political or ecclesiastical expediency, but a matter of life and death. Constantine wrote in threatening language to Athanasius, but for a time was himself cowed by the dauntless demeanour and replies of the young bishop. For some months the matter rested, while Eusebius and his Meletian allies were concocting a succession of charges against the motives, administration and character of Athanasius. They did not dare openly to assail his doctrines, lest they should bring upon themselves complicity with ideas which had been formally anathematized at Nicæa. It was enough if they could succeed in destroying the personal reputation of Athanasius with the Emperor, and thus compromise his position in the Church.

At this period in the episcopate of Athanasius must be placed the arrival in Alexandria of Frumentius, the Apostle of Ethiopia. Some critics find a hopeless chronological paradox in the statement both of Socrates and of Rufinus, that this visit occurred at the commencement of the episcopate of Athanasius; but the emphatic statements of the historians is curiously and decisively confirmed by an extant letter of Constantius to the kings of Ethiopia, preserved by Athanasius in his *Apology to Constantius*.[1] The story is given on the authority of Rufinus, who declares that he received it direct from one of the actors in the scene referred to. It runs as follows, and it throws a charming side-light upon the life of the Church in the fourth century —

An adventurous philosopher of the city of Tyre, Meropius by name, in the commencement of the century resolved on extensive travel, and took as his companions two well-instructed Christian youths, Frumentius and Ædesius. In some port on the Red Sea his vessel approached the shore to obtain food or water. The barbarians, who had recently thrown off all allegiance to the imperial power, fell upon the strangers, and massacred Meropius and the entire

[1] See article 'Ethiopian Church,' by the present writer, in *Dictionary of Christian Biography*, vol iii. 234-5.

crew of sailors and passengers, with the exception
of the two boys, who were found by the barbarous
people reading and praying under the shade of a
neighbouring tree. They were taken in triumph to
the king of the ancient city of Axum or Auxume, and
immediately secured his interest and affection. Their
accomplishments were prized by the monarch, who
made Ædesius his cupbearer and Frumentius his
secretary or treasurer. They became, as years passed,
the tutors of his two sons, the Atbreha and Atzbeha
of the Ethiopian annals The king died, and the
widowed queen besought them to remain with her
until her sons had reached man's estate, and to assist
her by their counsel in the affairs of her government.
They consented to do so, and lost no time in diffusing
some knowledge of the Gospel and in securing
privileges for Christian merchants who had found
their way into the country. By the zeal and sound-
ness of their faith they must have produced a very
wide-spread effect.

The seed sown sprang up rapidly, and the issue
must have corresponded with events of which we often
hear in the grand romance of modern missions. The
young evangelists and statesmen were eager to secure
greater privileges for their adopted country, and
sought opportunity to return to Christendom with
news of their spiritual success. In their early home,
Ædesius was persuaded to remain, and was ordained
as Presbyter of Tyre, and from him Rufinus heard the
story. Frumentius resolved to lay the whole details
before Athanasius at Alexandria, and to beseech him
to send a bishop to preside over the infant church in
Ethiopia. In a council of his presbyters, Athanasius
exclaimed, ' What other man shall we find such as
thou art, in whom is the Spirit of God as He is in

thee, who will be able to discharge these duties?'
The whole scene may be easily imagined. Frumentius
was consecrated first bishop of this unknown country.
The Ethiopian annals declare that when he returned
to the court of the barbarian kings apostolic signs
were wrought by his hands, and a vast number were
converted to the faith of Christ. He received the title
of *Abbuna,* or *Abba Salama,* ' *Father of Peace,*' and by
this name is known in the annals. The Metropolitan
of Auxume still bears this ancient name, and derives
his orders from the Patriarch of the Egyptian (Coptic)
Church.

In the stormy days of the life of Athanasius few
gleams of light resembling this broke athwart the
darkness. In subsequent years an effort was made to
damage the position of Frumentius by reason of the
orders he had received from the maligned and persecuted Bishop of Alexandria. But Arian doctrine and
tactics failed to produce any effect upon the Church of
Ethiopia. And now began the long and weary assault
upon the honour and character of Athanasius, which
for a while absorbed the attention of the world, and
cunningly concealed from view the magnitude of the
issue which was at stake. For a time the hostility of
the Eusebian party against Athanasius was allowed to
slumber, but the methods of their assault upon the
Catholic faith received painful and vivid exposition in
the treacherous course they pursued towards Eustathius, the honoured and beloved occupant of the
bishopric of Antioch. A hastily summoned synod of
bishops, led by Theognis and Eusebius of Cæsarea,
and assisted by his namesake of Nicomedia, met at
Antioch in A.D. 331,[1] accused the saintly man of pro-

[1] There is some controversy about the date, but the above
statement is supported by the best authorities.

fligacy, of disrespect to the mother of Constantine, of tyranny and of Sabellianism, and deposed him in his own palace, and compelled him to retire to Thrace. He never saw again the people of his charge, but died at Philippi in 337. The motive was clearly his powerful advocacy of the Nicene doctrine against Arian speculations, combined with personal dislike.

The animosity of the Meletians against Athanasius was stirred by the effort made by the bishop to bring them into the ecclesiastical order which they had defied. Eusebius of Nicomedia basely encouraged them to bring against Athanasius charges of malversation of government funds for the purchase of ecclesiastical vestments. These representations were made to the emperor by three Meletian bishops. The foul wrong was bitterly resented by the church at Antioch, and led to a schism which was not healed for a century. Fortunately, two Alexandrian priests at Nicomedia were able at once to disprove the malicious statements, and Constantine acquitted Athanasius of all fault, but summoned him to Nicomedia.

On the arrival of the bishop at Nicomedia, his enemies were ready with a succession of other accusations, which were disproved on the spot as wicked fabrications. A man named Ischyras had been ordained by a schismatic presbyter (not a bishop) to the pastorate of a little hamlet in the Mareotis. Athanasius sent one of his presbyters, Macarius, to administer rebuke to Ischyras for his uncanonical irregularities. The man was ill, and only received secondhand the injunction. On his recovery he naturally found sympathy among the Meletian partisans. Between them they trumped up the story that Macarius had sacrilegiously thrown down the Lord's table, broken the chalice, and burned the books; and that Athanasius was

responsible for the violence. Point by point these
charges were held to be absurd and untrue, if not
obviously vamped up to serve a purpose. Athanasius
(*Ap. c. Arianos*, §§ 11, 12) shows that Ischyras was no
presbyter, never having been ordained; that there was
no chalice to be broken and no church, and that at
the time of Macarius' visit there was 'no celebration
of the mysteries.' Moreover Ischyras confessed that
there was no truth whatever in the accusations, and
even sought communion with the church in Alexandria.
This, however, was not granted.

More desperate charges still were then concocted of
such atrocious kind that they appear to provoke their
own immediate refutation; yet hatred to the defender
of the Catholic faith led scores of Oriental bishops to
credit them for a while. Though absolutely disproved,
yet the defamatory and infamous charges still lingered
in the breasts of the enemies of Athanasius, and again
and again were hurled at him with bitter spite. John
Arcaph, the successor of Meletius in the see of Lycopolis, bribed a certain Arsenius to hide in some of the
monasteries of the Thebaid. Arcaph and his friends
then gave it out that the man had been murdered by
Athanasius! Moreover they pretended to have found
the right hand of Arsenius in a desiccated state, which
they brought in a box, exhibiting it as the instrument
which Athanasius had used for magical purposes.
Thus murder and magical arts were mendaciously
attributed to the brave young bishop. Even Constantine was staggered by the audacity of these charges,
and summoned Athanasius to take his trial at Antioch.
A chapter of curious accidents enabled the friends of
Athanasius to unearth the concealed Arsenius, who,
after at first denying his identity, was—in the presence
of Paul, the Bishop of Tyre, a man who knew him

personally—compelled to acknowledge the treacherous
design to which he had been a party. He and his
unprincipled leader, John Arcaph, confessed their
fault, first accepted the severe rebuke of Constantine,
and then sought fellowship and communion with
Athanasius. This was granted, and, as far as Arsenius
was concerned, was honourably maintained. During
the year 333 A.D. the Church and bishop were left in
peace, and the victories of Athanasius over pagans and
apostates were considerable.

An event of especial biographical interest occurred
during this year. The unchanged habits of the dwellers
in the valley of the Nile assist us vividly to realize
the journey of Athanasius to Upper Egypt in his Nile-
boat. Surrounded by a numerous suite of inferior
clergy and monks, he ascended the river, now sailing,
and now drawn forwards by his crew of Fellahin, past
the tombs of Beni-Hassan, the city of Lycopolis, the
temples of Abydos and Dendera, and the glories of
Thebes to Syene (Assouan) and the first cataract,
receiving everywhere the homage of the suffragan
bishops and troops of ascetics. At Tentyris (or Dendera)
Pachomius, an illustrious anchoret, hid himself
among his own followers and imitators, out of fear
that Athanasius might fasten upon him and force him
into the ranks of the priesthood. Pachomius gazed
with a kind of rapture on the bishop, but never discovered
himself, and the vessel stood forth into the
stream and vanished from their sight.

Such peaceful scenes as these seldom cheered the
great champion of the faith, nor can it be impugned
that in his vehement endeavour to bring the Meletians
and subscribing Arians into the unity of the Church
he may have used some violent measures. Callinicus,
Bishop of Pelusium, bitterly intrigued against Athana-

sius, and possibly provoked him by raking up the charge of his illegal appointment and uncanonical consecration. At all events, Athanasius unfrocked Callinicus, and used the secular power to carry out his decision.

During the year of peace the Eusebians were bringing every influence to bear upon Constantine to call a further synod or council at Cæsarea, to investigate more fully the numerous charges brought against Athanasius, and to secure the peace of the Church, in view of the approaching consecration of the great church built at Jerusalem in commemoration of our Lord's resurrection. Such an end would coincide with Constantine's darling project to proclaim a universal peace at the moment when he should celebrate his *tricennalia* on the thirtieth anniversary of his accession.

Such a council was held, and Athanasius was summoned to attend it, but refused. Thus his independent spirit roused still further the bitter animosity of his prejudiced judges and his declared enemies, by keeping them waiting and repudiating their authority for thirty months. The animosity of Eusebius, the Bishop of Cæsarea, was obviously known to the Emperor, and it may have been one reason which honourably moved him to summon a synod, to be held at Tyre, whose bishop, Paul, was known to be favourably disposed to the accused prelate; and to this synod was entrusted the duty of legally investigating the conduct of Athanasius. After some hesitation, Athanasius was compelled, in the summer of 335 A.D., to present himself at Tyre with forty-nine Egyptian bishops. But the Eusebian party was more numerous still, amounting to sixty bishops, including Eusebius of Cæsarea, and Eusebius of Nicomedia, Theognis and Maris, Valens and Ursacius.

Athanasius saw at once that all the dominant force of the assembly was pledged against him, from Flacillus of Antioch, who presided, and Count Flavius Dyonysius, who was the representative of the Emperor, an open enemy of Athanasius and violent partisan of the Eusebians, down to the rank and file of the Arianizers. The mind of Constantine must have been strongly moved at the time by the petition of Arius not only to be recalled from his exile, but, on the ground of his substantial orthodoxy, to be readmitted to the full communion of the Church. The Emperor could not see the defects of the statements of Arius, and handed the solution of this crucial question to the Cæsarean or Tyrian Council. The treatment to which Arius was to be submitted was to be placed in the hand of the council so soon as—having brought the Athanasian trouble to an end—it should be transferred to Jerusalem, to assist in the dedication of the church built on the site of the Holy Sepulchre.

The Council of Tyre was a scene of cruel vivacity and bitter recrimination. Athanasius found himself surrounded by unscrupulous enemies. They raised once more the ghost of Arsenius, and waved aloft the dismembered hand.

The treatment to which Arius was to be submitted was referred to the decision of the council.

Now Arsenius, whom the Meletians believed to be in hiding, but whom they frantically declared to have been murdered and mutilated by Athanasius, had been found in Lower Egypt, and conveyed in the suite of the bishop to the council. Athanasius calmly asked if any of the bishops present could recognise and identify Arsenius. On many affirmative replies being given, the man himself was brought before them, and proved to have both hands intact. Confusion and excitement prevailed, and John Arcaph left the assembly.

But, convincing and complete as this refutation was, the majority were so prejudiced against Athanasius that they attributed the scene under their very eyes to magical art. New charges of violence were brought against him, and he was treated as a common criminal, and made to stand as a prisoner at the bar of Eusebius of Cæsarea and others, who assumed the character of his accusers and his judges. Such indignity roused the ire of old Potammon of Heraclea, who had lost an eye in the persecution, and who did not scruple to charge Eusebius with having secured immunity from mutilation by unworthy compromise with heathen idolatry.

The venerable Paphnutius, from the Thebaid, with the hideous scar of his fierce conflict upon him, he of disfigured face and eye-socket, whom Constantine is said to have kissed with enthusiasm at the Council of Nicæa, was present, and produced a notable effect by drawing Maximus of Jerusalem (a fellow-sufferer with himself) out of the Arian cabal, which seemed thirsting for the disgrace if not for the destruction of Athanasius.

The enemies of Athanasius further raised the question of what they called his illegal election and consecration to the bishopric. On point after point Athanasius cleared himself. One of the charges was of a gross kind, and he was able triumphantly to vindicate his innocence, and expose the wicked machination which had concocted it. On the resuscitation of the old accusation, that in his violence Athanasius had broken a sacred chalice and overturned the table on which the Eucharist was being consecrated by Ischyras, fresh points were raised, to answer which it was

necessary to obtain time. The council appointed a
commission of six of the most bitter enemies of the
bishop to journey to the Mareotis and collect evidence
in support of the plea. This was so
transparently unjust that even Dionysius, under some
special pressure, endeavoured to restrain the violence
of the Eusebians.

Athanasius refused to accept the verdict of the
council, whatever it might prove to be, and resolved
to appeal to the Emperor in person. On this step,
upon which so much subsequently turned, arose one of
the most dramatic scenes in his life. The bishop, with
five of his friends, suddenly left Tyre by a vessel
starting for Constantinople. Meanwhile the council
proceeded to its foregone conclusion, and solemnly
and angrily deposed him from the see of Alexandria,
and recognised the Meletian bishops who refused his
authority as in full communion with the Church. They
then proceeded to Jerusalem, to assist in the dedication
of the church, and to adjudge that, according to
their light, Arius was an injured innocent, an orthodox
theologian, and on the faith of the Creed which he had
laid before Constantine to receive him into full communion.

Meanwhile, on one occasion, when the great Emperor
was, according to his wont, riding in his chariot in the
road between the palace and the city, Athanasius
suddenly presented himself, and demanded audience.
Ten years had passed over them both since they had
met in Nicæa. The lithe and vivacious form of the
young archdeacon had put on the signs of mature life
and burdensome care. Constantine was drawing near
his end, satiated with honours and successes and stained
with domestic crime. For the moment he failed to
recognise Athanasius, and refused to give him the

audience he demanded. But the bishop was not to be daunted, and with boldness of demeanour and elevated voice declared that he simply required justice. 'Let my accusers state their charges in thy presence. Be thou the judge between us.' Like Paul, when he became the victim of a merciless and bigoted cabal, Athanasius appealed to Cæsar. The Emperor wrote an almost apologetic letter to the members of the council, but demanded their presence at Constantinople. 'I,' said he, 'will judge of the equity of your decrees.' He claimed this power in virtue of the great prosperity God had granted to his arms and empire. 'We' (he added) 'ought not to do anything that can tend to dissension or hatred. . . . Come to us with all diligence, and be assured that I shall do everything in my power to preserve the inviolability of the law of God.'

Many of the council, alarmed at the tone of the Emperor, set off on their journey homewards; but the two Eusebii, Theognis, Patrophilus, Ursacius, and Valens, with others, presented themselves at Constantinople, and had at first the incredible baseness to ignore all the charges on the ground of which they had condemned Athanasius at Tyre, and to vamp up a fresh accusation, which they knew would rouse the suspicion of Constantine. They declared that in order to gain his purposes at Alexandria he had threatened to prevent the sailing of the Alexandrian corn-ships. They did not miscalculate the effect upon Constantine of this quasi-political crime. A fierce expression of wrath burst from the lips of the Emperor—whether simulated or genuine cannot be clearly ascertained. The very suspicion of any interference with imperial interests was enough. The defence made by Athanasius was not listened to. When he declared

his entire inability to effect anything of the kind, even
if he had the will, Eusebius of Nicomedia, with an
oath, replied that his victim was a man of vast wealth
and influence, and could, if he pleased, have stopped
the supplies of corn to the imperial treasuries. His
fate was sealed. 'He sent me away to Gaul,' is the
touching language of Athanasius (*Ap. c. Ar.*, § 87). It
is true that Sozomen (ii. 28) speaks of the introduction
of the absurd charges about the chalice, but, as Tillemont suggests, this may easily have been done after
Constantine's mind was made up.

In the letter which the younger Constantine sent to
the people of the Catholic Church in Alexandria in
338, he says that 'Athanasius had been sent away into
Gaul for a time, with the intent that as the savageness
of his bloodthirsty and inveterate enemies persecuted
him to the hazard of his sacred life, he might thus
escape suffering some irremediable calamity, through
the perverse dealing of these evil men' (*Ap. c. Ar.*, § 87).
Constantine, like Napoleon, could simulate wrath, and
was a dexterous politician. He may have acted on
this occasion from blended and even opposing motives.

CHAPTER VI.

ATHANASIUS IN EXILE AT TRÈVES (TRIER), AND WHAT HAPPENED IN THE INTERIM.

THE celebrated city of Trèves, which in its own legends
boasts a greater antiquity than Rome itself, was the
early seat of the strong tribe of Germanized Gauls,
or Celts, called Treveri, who gradually fell under the
expanding dominion of the imperial city. In the early

days of the empire, it acquired the name and the privileges of a Roman colony. Its fortress and camp marked the border-land between Gaul, Roman and Teuton. Here Rome stood firmly, and resolved to hold her own. A mixed population tenanted the city, part of which spoke, even in Jerome's day, the very dialect heard in Galatia; another part yielded to the fascination of Greek, while the majority were familiar with the language of Rome and boasted of Roman citizenship.

'Rome (says Mr. Freeman)[1], as an imperial dwelling-place, gave way to points better suited to command the threatened frontiers, to Milan, to Nikomêdia, to Antioch, and the new Rome herself.' Trèves (Trier) became 'the point chosen for the defence of Gaul against the German, the capital of the West, the centre of dominion for Gaul, Spain and Britain, the second Rome beyond the Alps.' There, on the banks of the Mosel, Diocletian and Maximian celebrated their brotherhood as twin Augusti of the Roman world. In the extant panegyrics, Maximian's residence at Trèves is described with effusion, and so are the marvellous buildings erected by Constantius I. and Constantine. The *circus* almost equalled that of Rome. The majestic basilica rivalled in vastness, if not in splendour and ornament, the basilicas of Rome, and now in this nineteenth century it has been at length transformed into a Christian church. Here, too, stood the stupendous amphitheatre, and in the reign of Constantine gladiatorial shows were celebrated on a colossal scale. In the early years of that reign captive kings were slaughtered for the amusement of the grateful people; and the panegyrists never tire of extolling the

---

[1] 'Augusta Treverorum,' *British Quarterly Review*, July, 1875.

hideous brutality which still formed the excitement of the mercurial Celt and hardened Roman. Legend refers the vast *Porta Nigra*, or Black Gate, to prehistoric workmen. The huge stones were held together by clamps of iron, and Oriental builders have been supposed necessary to account for its obvious characteristics. Mr. Freeman inclines to the belief that it indicates separate and successive stages, and that its upper stories and Romanesque arches belong to the latest period of Roman domination.

To Trèves Constantine had brought the body of his mother, Helena, and buried it with great pomp; and in the later days of his reign churches were in process of erection. The celebrated metropolitan church had not yet been built; but there were, without doubt, churches where the Court of the Cæsar worshipped. Agrætius, the bishop from A.D. 313 to 332, was present at the Council of Arles. Maximinus and Paulinus occupied the see in succession to him.

Here, about the month of February, A.D. 336, Athanasius arrived. He found Constantine II., the eldest son of the great Emperor, conducting as Cæsar the affairs of the Roman government. Though far aloof from the controversies of the East and the sufferings of his own flock, the illustrious exile found congenial friendship in the person of the orthodox bishop Maximinus, and the kindly care of the Cæsar, who accepted his doctrine and appreciated his character and virtues. One may even trace to his influence the introduction into the Western Church of the principle and laws of ascetic self-renunciation, which, though they had run to great extremes in the Nitrian desert and in the valley of the Nile, assumed nobler form when the idea took possession of the more phlegmatic temperament and practical energies of the West.

IN EXILE AT TRÈVES.

Without discussing the vexed question of the authorship of *The Life of St. Anthony*, which is referred by many traditional testimonies to Athanasius, without endorsing even the historical character of the life or work of this remarkable personage, we think it obvious, from the *Confessions* of Augustine, that the religious circles in Trèves had been strongly moved by the self-abandonment and entire consecration to the 'religious life' of the exiled bishop. It was here, while reading *The Life of St. Anthony*, that the friends of Augustine at length yielded themselves to God, the story of which led him to break away from his sinful compliances, and at length to resolve on a step of such transcendent interest to the whole Church of God.[1] It was from Trèves that Athanasius wrote some of his *Festal Letters*, which kept alive the flame of affection for himself in the hearts of his widowed flock. It was here he must have heard, from time to time, as he passed the banks of the gleaming Mosel or glanced on

[1] See August., *Conf.*, Lib. viii 6. Dr Newman believes in the 'substantial integrity' of the Life. Gregory of Nazianzus knew of the book, and Chrysostom and Augustine quote it without mentioning the writer, yet there is grave reason for doubting the authorship by Athanasius. He never elsewhere alludes to Anthony except in the reference to one story, of which he gives, however, a discrepant account. Some modern writers (see Mr Gwatkin's *Studies in Arianism*; Arch. Farrar, *Cont. Rev.*, Nov., 1887) incline to the belief that the entire story is a romance in illustration of an ideal, and which became so popular as to excite a wide-spread belief in the historic existence of Anthony. We are loth to give up the pretty story of Athanasius pouring water on the hands of the old recluse, or the halo of sanctity that preserved him from his foes in the Maximian persecution, or the enthusiasm with which he is said, in his extreme age, to have maintained the cause of Athanasius; or that he came to Alexandria to protest against the conduct of the Arians during the Council of Tyre.

the crowds in the huge amphitheatre, the thrilling record of the affairs of the Eastern Church and Empire. Let us review some of these.

(1) The solemn dedication of the Church of the Holy Sepulchre.—The supposed site of the Sepulchre of our Lord at Jerusalem had been discovered, as it was thought; and Constantine's mother, Helena, in her enthusiasm for holy things and places, sought to erect over it, in lieu of a polluting temple of Venus which had been reared on the spot, a temple of the Lord, in honour alike of His cruel death and His glorious resurrection. Constantine urged forward the completion of a building described in glowing terms by Eusebius (*Vita Cons.*, iii. 33-42) and Sozomen (ii. 26). The atrium, with its 'gates of exquisite workmanship' and 'numberless offerings of inexpressible beauty,' 'the floor of marble slabs of various colours,' 'the roof finished with sculptured fretwork, extended like a vast canopy over the whole church, which was overlaid throughout with purest gold, and which caused the entire building to glitter as with rays of light.' The idea of the temple in Jerusalem was re-embodied, from its open courts to its sanctuary, where 'an altar in a vast apse was enriched by twelve columns, and their capitals embellished with drums of silver.' The melancholy beginning here reveals itself of that abolition of true equality in the company of the faithful people, and of the growth and intensity of the bastard sacerdotalism which has done so much to limit and quench the power of the Holy Spirit in the Church.

Athanasius himself thought less than did many of his contemporaries of the sacredness of places, and all the pomp of the dedication of the Church must have palled upon his spirit. On a subsequent occasion he was accused of thinking and acting as though he utterly undervalued the ceremonial sanctity of places, and in his *Apologia ad Constantium*, § 17, he vindicated himself by the authority of the blessed Master Himself.

While this dedication was proceeding in 335, the Eusebian and Arian bishops held their unholy synod, at which they enunciated a blank contradiction to the Nicæan formulary, and decided that the profession of faith handed in by Arius himself was satisfactory to them. It was an artfully composed document, which had a show of orthodoxy, but dexterously omitted all reference to the burning question of the *homoousion*, and left open the dispute between the opposed parties. The Emperor imagined that it was identical with the Creed of Nicæa, and the bishops assembled at Jerusalem either took their cue from him or were incapable of rightfully estimating the conditions of the problem. The issue was that they wrote to the Emperor, to the churches of Alexandria, of Thebes, and of Libya, beseeching them to receive Arius and Euzoius back into communion. This fearful blow must have fallen upon the exile at Trèves very soon after his arrival.

(2) A synod was called at Constantinople of the Eusebian faction who had just effected the exile of Athanasius; and here the tactics of the party were clearly revealed. They had not dared to accuse Athanasius of doctrinal error or 'impiety,' knowing well that the charge would recoil upon their own heads, and they consequently sought and contrived to eject him from his see by cruel charges against his moral character, his canonical position, and his political loyalty. But the celebrated Galatian bishop, Marcellus, was a target against whom they could launch their charge of heterodoxy; and one of the chief acts of the synod was to move once more against him. This Marcellus (of Ancyra) offended them by his vigorous

attempt to refute an Arian disputant. He had, however, done this so injudiciously that he had really laid himself open to a charge of heresy. Grave difference of opinion has always prevailed as to the precise nature of his views. By the Eusebian party Marcellus was accused of Sabellianism, although he strenuously denied the imputation. It is true that he repudiated the idea of the eternal generation of the Son, and confined himself to an assertion of the eternal immanence of the Logos in God, and of the creative energy of the Logos in all things as well as in the person of Christ. 'The Logos,' said he, 'could only be said to be *begotten* when miraculously conceived in the womb of His mother. The Sonship of the *Christ* began on His manifestation in the flesh.' He tried thus to sever the knot which the conservative party in the Church had tied unwittingly, when it found itself pledged at one and the same time to the unity of God, to the Divinity of the Christ, and to the veritable humanity of Jesus. He fell back upon the Philonic conception of the Logos as the sole explanation of the *Divinity* of Christ and His pre-existence. He sacrificed both the personality of the Logos and even the human personality of Jesus, and the result was profoundly unsatisfactory. Under shelter of the Nicene formularies, he seemed to have fallen back on the heresy of Paul of Samosata, and to have anticipated that of Apollinaris. When the Eusebians met in council at Constantinople, they probably had little difficulty in condemning and dispossessing the Bishop of Ancyra. This news, aggravated by the circumstance that Marcellus had stood bravely by the side of Athanasius when contesting the Arian hypothesis, must have reached our illustrious exile.

(3) The death of Arius.—For the dramatic incidents

of this tragic event we are mainly indebted to the Epistle of Athanasius (written many years afterwards) to Serapion the monk. They must have been related to Athanasius by his friend Macarius, the presbyter, who was eye-witness of the strange ending of the notorious heresiarch (*Epis. ad. Ser*, § 2). By the insistence of the Eusebians, Arius was summoned by the Emperor into his presence, and was asked whether he held the Catholic faith. He appealed to the specious document which had been regarded as satisfactory by the synod at Jerusalem. He swore with a mighty oath that he did not profess the opinions for which Alexander of Alexandria had excommunicated him. Constantine dismissed him, saying: 'If thy faith be right, thou hast done well to swear; but if thy faith be impious (heretical), and thou hast sworn, God judge thee according to thy oath.'[1] The Eusebians declared to the aged Alexander of Constantinople that, whether contrary to his desire or not, on the next day Arius should commune with them in the metropolitan church. The bishop cast himself upon the floor of the chancel and prayed with his face to the ground, and Macarius heard him say, 'If Arius be brought to communion to-morrow, let me Thy servant depart this life; but if Thou wilt spare Thy Church, look upon the words of the Eusebians, and give not Thine inheritance to destruction and reproach, and take off Arius.' While the Eusebians threatened, the bishop prayed on, like Hezekiah when the armies of Sennacherib were round about Jerusalem. But Arius talked very wildly, and, urged by the necessities of nature, withdrew, and suddenly 'falling head-

---

[1] Cf. *Encyc. Epistle*, ii. 13, Soz., *H. E.*, ii. 30, which gives merely a quotation from the letter of Athanasius.

long, he burst asunder in the midst, and immediately expired as he lay, and was deprived both of communion and of his life together.'

Athanasius repudiates all glorying in the death, but he not unnaturally regarded it as a direct Divine interposition. 'The Lord Himself condemned the heresy which rose up against Him.' We dare not, with our Lord's weighty words (Luke xiii. 1-5) before us and the entire teaching of Scripture, come to any such conclusion from the tragic termination of the career of Arius. It cannot be doubted, however, that such a thrilling event as this, happening at such a moment in the history of the conflict, deepened its intensity and aggravated the feelings of the combatants.

(4) The death of Constantine the Great.—Neither the death of Arius nor the vehement protests of the church in Alexandria produced any effect upon the mind of Constantine; nor did he, in consequence, obviously relent in his determination to prolong the exile of Athanasius, but apparently continued to regard him as a dangerous, turbulent, and seditious man. He divided the immense empire among his sons. To Constantine II. and Constans he assigned the Western world, and to Constantius II. the Eastern provinces. A fatal illness now seized him, and, after reaching Nicomedia, he offered himself for baptism. He put off his purple robe of sovereignty, and was clothed with the white garments of the Christian neophyte. He was filled (it is said) with great joy. He is reported to have placed his last instructions in the hand of an Arian priest. Not one of his sons was at his side. He died in the sixty-fifth year of his age and the thirty-first of his reign, at noon on the day of Pentecost, in the year 337. His body was placed in a golden coffin, conveyed to Constantinople, and deposited in the palace

DEATHS OF ARIUS AND CONSTANTINE.

until the youthful Constantius arrived, when it was interred, amid prodigious pomp, in the Church of the Apostles.[1]

This is not the place to estimate the character or life-work of Constantine. In the eloquent words of Dean Stanley,[2] 'So passed away the first Christian emperor, the first Defender of the Faith, the first imperial patron of the papal see and of the whole Eastern Church, the first founder of the Holy Places, Pagan and Christian, orthodox and heretical, liberal and fanatical, not to be imitated or admired, but much to be remembered and deeply to be studied.' Mr. Gwatkin[3] observes: 'Darkly as his memory is stained with isolated crimes, Constantine must for ever rank among the greatest of the emperors. . . . Others equalled—few surpassed—his gifts of statesmanship and military genius, and as an actual benefactor to mankind Constantine stands almost alone in history.'

This lofty approval is based upon the new weapon which Christianity placed in the hands of the great commander, to promote the peace of the world and to strike a blow at its social evils, and on the manner in which he wielded it. The blending of the sacred and secular powers, though it liberated the martyr Church from its secret hiding-places, and exalted the new faith to the throne of the world, yet introduced a novel and mundane element into its spiritual life. It lent the secular arm to a triumphant hierarchy, fearfully invaded the sanctuary, breathed a more bitter animosity into the struggles of rival ecclesiastics and contending formularies, and prepared the way for the intolerance and religious persecution of later centuries.

[1] Eusebius, *Vita Cons.*, iv. 63–74.
[2] *Eastern Church*, p. 259.
[3] *Studies of Arianism*, p. 106.

62   *ATHANASIUS.*

The death of Constantine the 'Great' did not terminate the exile of the Bishop of Alexandria. It remained to be seen whether the sympathies of the new Augusti were with Athanasius or with his enemies. The exile must have been able to count upon the favour of Constantine II., but Constantius II. was master of the Eastern world, and this prince rapidly revealed his alliance with the Eusebian party and manifested a deadly animosity to Athanasius.

CHAPTER VII.

THE RETURN OF ATHANASIUS FROM HIS FIRST EXILE, AND THE COMMENCEMENT OF THE SECOND.

CONSIDERABLE controversy has prevailed with reference to the *date* of the release of Athanasius from Trèves: whether it occurred in the autumn of 337 or the summer of 338. Ceillier, Tillemont, J. H. Newman, Hefele, and Bright accept the latter date, on the ground of the fact that Constantine II., on the 17th of the month of June (not mentioning the year), and *after* the death of his father, wrote the letter granting the privilege of his release from Trèves. They think that the news of the death of the great Emperor could not have reached Constantine the younger so soon as June 19th, 337, and therefore suppose the letter to have been written in June, 338. If this were the case, the suspense of the exile must have been prolonged during thirteen weary months. Mr. Gwatkin has ably combated the supposition that the news of the death of Constantine could not have reached Trevès by June

19th of 337, and urges that Athanasius might and could have met the three emperors in the autumn of 337. This, moreover, is the date given in the *Festal Letter* of 338, and was that assumed by Valesius.

There is, however, no doubt that, in obedience to the presumed desire of their father, the three emperors, on the instigation of Constantine II., allowed Athanasius to return to his see. His arrival at Alexandria in the autumn of 337 or summer of 338 was the occasion of much rejoicing among the Egyptian bishops and the city population which had remained faithful to him. Gregory of Nazianzus, speaking of the spontaneous outburst of enthusiasm in tropical language, stated that so vast was the concourse, 'it was as if the Nile, at the height of its flood, scattering fertility as it went, had turned its course and flowed backwards from Alexandria to the first outpost of the city.' He compared it to Christ's triumphal entry into Jerusalem. 'There was one long unbroken shout of applause; the city at night flashed with illuminations, and a marvellous accession was made to the numbers of those who accepted the ascetic life.'[1]

The Eusebian party were, however, roused into a very lively antagonism, and once more used treacherous and lying calumnies to depreciate the character of Athanasius in the view of the emperors, and especially of Constantius, who was leaning more and more to the conservative party, and imbibing a hatred of the Nicene Confession. Moreover they began to accuse him of misappropriating the grain designed for charity in the Libyan province, and of having, by the mere favour of the secular power, set at nought the deposition of the Council of Tyre, and resumed his occu-

---

[1] Greg. Naz., *Orat* 28.

pancy of the see without the sanction of the council.
They went a step further, and did what would not
have been permissible in the reign of Constantine.
They appointed a notorious Arian presbyter, Pistus by
name, as bishop of the Arian party in Alexandria. He
was consecrated by Secundus, one of the bishops who
had been deposed at the Council of Nicæa ; and thus
the attempt was made to establish a permanent schism
in the Church.

They did more still: they sent an envoy to the
Roman Bishop Julius, to secure his countenance for
their nominee, and to place before him in most
malevolent form all the charges early and late that
had been fabricated against Athanasius. He, however,
called at Alexandria a notable synod of more
than one hundred bishops.[1] These bishops entirely
exonerated Athanasius of every one of the charges ;
and when their letters and papers were laid before the
Roman Julius, the Eusebian representatives were
obviously confounded by their own shame, and feebly
asked Julius to convene another council, over which
he should preside in person. Julius consented, and
invited both parties to assemble at a synod to be held
at some place which Athanasius should choose.

Meanwhile, either in the winter of 339-40 or in that
of 338-39,[2] the Eusebians held a council at Antioch,

[1] This synod must have been held in 338 *or* 339. Constans,
Constantine II., and Constantius II. were then living The two
former are stated by Athanasius himself (*Hist. Arian.*, c. 9)
to have credited his envoys, and dismissed his accusers with
disgrace.

[2] The *Festal Letters* of Athanasius, recently translated from
the Syriac, explicitly state that in 339 Athanasius fled from
Alexandria on Phamenoth xxii., four days before Gregory
entered the city as bishop, so that the earlier date is now
probable. See translation, p xviii.

where Constantius had fixed his headquarters. This council is not to be confounded with the 'Council of Dedication,' as is done by Socrates and Sozomen. At this synod they formally deposed Athanasius, and appointed, not Pistus, the Arian bishop, but, with approval of Constantius, one Gregory of Cappadocia to the vacant see. With the aid of soldiery, under the direction and sanction of the prefect Philagrius, the most hideous and atrocious cruelties were practised. The sacred elements were dishonoured, the virgins were stripped and beaten, the holy books were burned, the churches and the baptistries became the scene of foul and heathenish orgies. Similar violence was shown to the friends of Athanasius in other parts of Egypt. Potammon, the celebrated bishop and confessor, was so cruelly beaten that he ultimately 'died of his maltreatment and attained in Christ to the glory of a second martyrdom.'[1] Holy women were sold into slavery, publicly whipped, and banished from their homes. The orphans and widows of the Church were deprived of the bread devoted to their use, and every possible indignity was heaped on the Athanasian party.

Athanasius disappeared on March 19th, 339-40, before the violence had reached its height, and in the month of April sailed to Rome, whither he was followed by Marcellus of Ancyra and other ecclesiastics who had been exiled by the Eusebian party. The violence of the Eusebians was perhaps stimulated by the fratricidal war raging between Constans and Constantine II., which issued in the death of the latter. The *Encyclical Epistle* of Athanasius describes these calamities in great detail, and shows how, during his

[1] This terrible recital is given in detail by Athanasius himself, in his *Arian History*, §§ 9-13.

absence in Rome, the Alexandrine and Egyptian churches were summoned to come into communion with Gregory. They, however, preferred to deprive themselves of all Christian ordinances rather than receive them at the hands of their cruel persecutor, —the heterodox usurper of the episcopate.

Athanasius found numerous friends in Rome; among them a sister of the great Constantine. Julius received the exiles with respect, judicially reserving his opinion until the charges against them had been investigated. Meanwhile the envoys of the Roman bishop—who bore to Antioch a summons to the council, the convening of which the Eusebians had desired— could extract no answer from them. They probably felt that the presence of Athanasius in Rome would powerfully militate against and neutralize their contention. So they kept the envoys waiting in Antioch until January, 340—when they were scornfully dismissed.

Hefele and Bright have reconstructed the gist of their communication from the reply of Julius.[1] The Eusebians must have rested their case (*a*) on the deposition of Athanasius at the Council of Tyre, which, as they urged, would not suffer any reconsideration without impairing the validity of councils altogether. Julius showed that the decisions of the Council of Nicæa itself had provided for such a case, and at the Council of Tyre the Eusebians had themselves endeavoured to reverse the Nicene condemnation of the Arian formulary and professors. (*b*) They pleaded that the autumn of the year was much too soon for such an assembly, in consequence of the

---

[1] This reply is preserved at length in the *Apolog. c. Arianos*, §§ 21–35.

Persian war, a position which Julius declared to be a flimsy and transparent subterfuge for their non-appearance. (c) They urged that Julius had no right to summon them to Rome—that one bishop was as good as another, and did not derive his authority from the importance of his see. Julius twitted them in reply for not acting on their own principle. He asked them why Eusebius of Nicomedia had sought and obtained the archbishopric of Constantinople? (d) They urged further that Julius should not have written merely to the Eusebian party, but to all the bishops assembled at Antioch. Julius said in reply, 'There is in this objection more of readiness to find fault than of regard for truth.' He had simply written to those who had written to him; then he proceeded to inform them that the sentiments he had expressed were those of a council of fifty bishops, who assembled in Rome itself at the time he had appointed for them, and that they had unanimously come to the conclusion that the charges brought against Athanasius and Marcellus were absolutely false. He temperately summed up the stories about Arsenius and Ischyras, the injustice of the proceedings on the Mareotic commission (*see* pages 49, 50), and the proof of the canonical consecration of Athanasius in 326. For eighteen months Athanasius had been detained in Rome, but was proved to deserve the fullest confidence of the Roman see, and his character to contrast forcibly with the unheard-of violence with which his enemies had forced upon the people of Alexandria a bishop whom the Egyptian believers abhorred and with whom they dared not commune.

The vindication of Marcellus followed, which perhaps is not so satisfactory. Anyhow, Julius could not detect his heterodoxy, and cited his repudiation of

Arianism, which he assumes that the Eusebians were also prepared to make. He declared that numerous other bishops and presbyters had been treated with similar opprobrium and cruelty on their part, giving most crushing evidence to sustain his judgment. He charged upon them the flame of discord which had sprung up, and concluded with a powerful practical appeal to their honour.

The letter of Julius finally referred to the fact that the bishops were once more on the point of reassembling at Antioch. This reference is explained by the fact, that in the year 341 the Synod of Antioch *in encæniis* (ἐγκανίοις) was held. It was an expansion or development of the previous Antiochian synod, and was of a more catholic character. The special duty was conferred upon it of dedicating the new and gorgeous church which Constantine I. had initiated and his son Constantius completed. Great perplexity has arisen from the circumstance that a council, the main purpose of which appears to have been the confirmation of the deposition of Athanasius and the passing of several declarations of belief all more or less speciously orthodox, yet aiming at the obliteration of the specialities of the Nicæan formulary, and containing a distinct condemnation of Julius for his vindication of Marcellus, should nevertheless have been regarded by the Church as of indubitable authority, and should have established certain ecclesiastical canons which were subsequently accepted by the Œcumenical Councils.

One plausible interpretation of the mystery is, that the notorious twenty-five canons were passed immediately after the consecration of the church at the commencement of the council by the majority of the bishops who were in these early sessions; that these bishops were distinctly orthodox, conservative, and anti-Arian, and that after this duty was discharged they departed. It is supposed that the deposition of Athanasius and the theological discussions that followed were the work of an Arian cabal, who chose to act upon the force of a canon which they contrived to pass with the distinct purpose of assailing the position of Athanasius.

This plausible suggestion is scarcely justified on close examination of the four creeds which were passed by the council. There is no material distinction in their spirit, but each labours with extreme ingenuity to approach as closely as possible to the Nicene formulary without using the term *Homoousios* or *Homoiousios* ('of the same' or 'of a similar substance' with the Father.) They were drawn up by the Eusebians with the view of securing the votes of the conservatives. Hilary does not condemn the second of the formularies, which was based upon the creed of Lucian, the martyred bishop, and interprets it in the orthodox sense. Even Athanasius does not declare them positively heretical.

The difficulty may be reduced by observing the fact that the stories concerning Athanasius had never been eradicated from the minds of the majority, that the partially informed were deceived by the passionate partisans of Eusebius of Nicomedia into acquiescence, and that there must have been certain reported actions of Athanasius which were never cleared up to their satisfaction.

When the deposition of the prelate and the pseudo-accurate Creed of Antioch, No. IV., were laid by the Arians before Constans, his reply was in 343 a summons of Athanasius from Rome to Milan.

Meanwhile the Eusebians, who had drawn up yet

another creed, called from its great elaboration (Macrostich) 'the long-lined confession,' presented this to the Western bishops assembled at Milan. It produced no impression on them, and was felt to be an attempt to evade the teaching of the Nicene formulary.

On his arrival, Athanasius found that Constans had already agreed with his brother Constantius to summon a council of the bishops both of the Eastern and Western Churches to adjudicate on his position and to place the synod, moreover, under the impartial presidency of the venerable Hosius of Cordova.

CHAPTER VIII.

THE COUNCIL OF SARDICA AND THE SECOND RETURN OF ATHANASIUS.

THE site of the council was on the border-line between the two empires, at SARDICA[1] in Mœsia, but within the territory of the Western emperor, Constans. Bishops to the number of 170 assembled, and the majority were Western and Athanasian in their sympathies. The Arian or semi-Arian party were thus baffled in their tactics. Conjoint action was impossible, as the Western bishops persisted in ignoring the *ex parte* statements of the Antiochian Council and the prejudgment of the case of Athanasius, Paul and Marcellus. The Eusebians demanded the expulsion of the inculpated bishops, as persons already excommunicated, and, shutting themselves up in one house in the town of Sardica, refused

---

[1] Now called Sophia.

THE COUNCIL OF SARDICA.

every injunction and every entreaty to join the Western bishops in their fresh investigation *de novo* of all the charges which had been so recklessly brought against Athanasius. They had abundant reason to fear that the tables would be turned against them. Witnesses of their cruelty to the Alexandrine clergy were in attendance. The instruments of torture used by their representatives to compel communion with their nominee, Gregory, and letters which were manifestly forged, with the view of prejudicing the minds of the emperors, were in the possession of the friends of Athanasius; and so the Eusebians, but with obvious cowardice, shrank from the conflict with their illustrious victim in a purely ecclesiastical assembly. They had reason to fear their own failure, to dread the presentation of damning proofs of their scandalous intrigue; and so, under pretence of meeting Constantius on his return from the Persian war, they hastily withdrew by night, and proceeded to hold on Eastern territory, in the city of Philippopolis, a rival council of their own, where they incriminated Hosius and Julius, fiercely reasserted their Antiochian condemnation of Athanasius and Marcellus, and published a fifth creed, which closely resembled the fourth Creed of Antioch,—one which, while studiously avoiding the *Homoousios*, also repudiated the strong phrases of the strict Arians. They did even worse, for they endeavoured to deceive the Eastern Churches by their encyclical letter from Sardica. Whether this was of *malice prepense*, or whether by a self-mystification they regarded themselves as the true Council of Sardica, cannot be determined; but that they did practically deceive and mislead North African and Donatist bishops into this belief is unquestioned. Hefele (*Hist. of Councils*, iii. 172, E. T.) takes the more lenient view.

Meanwhile the Western bishops, representing thirty-five provinces of the empire, persisted in a thorough investigation into the entire proceedings of Athanasius, and abundantly acquitted him of every charge. So far as they had power of restoring him to his see, from which he had been ejected with violence, they did what was possible to them, and formulated their opinion with the utmost celerity, fulness, and force. They addressed letters to the church of Alexandria, to the bishops of Egypt and Libya, and also an encyclical letter to the whole Church, in each of which they controvert the charges and malicious slanders of the Eusebian party, press the cordial reception of their beloved fellow-bishop, Athanasius, into the fullest confidence and communion, and also make arrangements by which those who were unable to attend the synod should yet be able to express their coincidence with the unanimous conclusions of the Fathers of Sardica.[1] Accordingly, Athanasius[2] enumerated the names of no fewer than 344 or 347 in all, who stood boldly in his defence and on the side of his acquittal.

The Eusebian party obviously made a series of tactical and inept mistakes in their entire management of the Sardican Council, which may be partly due to the circumstance that they had lost their leader. Eusebius of Nicomedia had recently died. The atrocious way—too gross for recital—in which Stephen, the Arianized Bishop of Antioch, treated the two delegates who were sent A.D. 344 from the Council of Sardica to make known its decisions, led to a temporary reaction in favour of Athanasius, and even to the deposition of Stephen. This proceeding of Stephen began to open the eyes of Constantius to the *malice prepense* of the

[1] All these letters are preserved, *Apol c. Ar.*, §§ 36–49.
[2] *Ibid*, § 50

THE COUNCIL OF SARDICA.

Arian leaders. Moreover the death—not impossibly the murder—of the tyrannous Gregory by some of his exasperated flock in 345 (Tillemont says, 349) certainly cleared the way for the reinstating of Athanasius in his see. The decisions of Sardica were indisputable and widely circulated; Constans warmly espoused his cause, and threatened to involve the empire in civil war rather than submit to the continued exile of Athanasius.

Constantius yielded at length, and for a while appeared to coincide in the decision of the Council of Sardica, and wrote three [1] letters of exceeding unction to Athanasius, calling him his most beloved father, giving him permission to return to Alexandria, facilitating his travel, and enjoining on all the authorities respectful treatment. Constantius begged Athanasius to visit him; and these two men did meet for the third and last time at Antioch.[2] Before doing so, however, Athanasius returned to Rome to take farewell of Julius, had an interview with Constans at Adrianople, and thus kept Constantius waiting for the meeting referred to for a whole year. At length, however, he left Antioch on a visit to Maximus at Jerusalem, where a synod was held, which coincided with the decisions of Sardica; and his way homeward, October, 346, was rendered felicitous by the enthusiasm and affection of the Bishops of Libya and Palestine and of the province of Alexandria. It is not improbable that Gregory of Nazianzus, in his brilliant panegyric, recounted the

---

[1] These letters are preserved, *Apol. c. Ar*, §§ 54, 55.

[2] Philostorgius (III. 12) gives a very different account of the interview, and of the cordiality that prevailed between them. According to him, the permission to return was extorted by fear of Constans' threat to enforce it by armed intervention on political rather than religious grounds, Constantius regarding the restoration as the least of two evils.

circumstances of this second return, though in referring it, with Stanley, to the first return (p. 63), we are influenced chiefly by the silence of Athanasius himself on this matter.[1] He says nothing of a triumphal entry, and instead of this calls attention to the moral and spiritual results of his restoration, and to the fresh impetus given to the 'religious' life on the part of maidens and youths. He mentions also the almost fiery enthusiasm of piety and charity, 'so that you would have thought every family and every house to be a church, by reason of the goodness of its inmates and the prayers which were offered to God.'

CHAPTER IX.

THE RESUMPTION OF THE ARIAN PERSECUTION AND THE THIRD EXILE.

The bishops everywhere wrote to their metropolitan letters of joy and gratitude, and received answers of peace. Ursacius and Valens professed their entire reconciliation, rejected the charges of the Arian party, and asked for communion with the Church, in an extant letter to Julius of Rome. In the Festal Letter of 347,[2] Athanasius thanks God that he has been 'brought back (after eight years) from distant lands;' and he shortly afterwards held a synod to confirm in Africa the Sardican creed and canons. More than 400 bishops in all parts of the Western and Eastern

[1] *Arian History*, § 25
[2] This date, so emphatically given in Festal Letter xix., is accepted also by Gwatkin, Bright and Hefele.

empires openly expressed their sympathy with him. Numerous churches which had been filled by Arians were once more occupied by those who professed the Catholic faith. He was subsequently charged by the Arians with having on this occasion exercised episcopal functions beyond his own jurisdiction. This is far from probable, as in his apology he makes no reference to the charge.

For a few years, his renown was greater, his influence more penetrating, than ever; the success of his plans was assured by the support given to him by the Emperor of the West and by the silence or neutrality of Constantius. But a terrible blow was once more about to descend upon him and the Nicene orthodoxy. In the year 350 an event of tragic colour and ultimately of grave importance to Athanasius occurred. The moral character of the Emperor Constans was degraded in the eyes of his own generals by criminal and revolting practices. Magnentius, an 'ambitious soldier of fortune,' and probably of Gallic origin, secured, by bribery and promises, the allegiance and devotion of an important band of imperial troops, who suddenly hailed him as Augustus and Imperator, took the oath of fidelity to him, and helped him to become master of Autun. Constans fled, and before he could find protection in Spain became a victim to the ambition of the usurper, and by the hands of his representatives fell, at the foot of the Pyrenees. Other cities, camps, and provinces admitted the sovereignty of Magnentius, who thus became, by favour of the soldiery, Augustus of Italy and Gaul.

The example of rebellion was contagious, and Vetranio, an old general attached to the family of Constantine, was seduced by Constantina (the sister of Constans and Constantius) to accept the imperial diadem from her hands. Vetranio entered into ignoble alliance with Magnentius, and the two upstarts sent ambassadors to treat with Constantius, who had hurried from the disasters of the Persian campaign to face the perils of a civil war nearer the central seats of empire. Constantius refused to treat with Magnentius, and by a show of conciliation with Vetranio disentangled him from the alliance with the murderer of his brother. At Sardica a solemn farce was enacted, by which Vetranio abdicated his supposed authority, and retired into privacy, leaving Constantius free to wrest from Magnentius the power he had won by treachery and bloodshed. It was not, however, until August, 353, after a lengthened campaign, after numerous battles and various fortunes, that Magnentius fell upon his own sword, and Constantius became sole ruler of the Roman empire.

These tragic events exercised a very disastrous effect upon the career of Athanasius. The death of Constans deprived the bishop of the temporal support of the Emperor of the West; and though Constantius assured him that no peril awaited him, and even wrote to him advising him to continue his episcopal duties,[1] yet the Arian friends of Constantius soon endeavoured to mystify and deceive him as to the feelings, purposes and policy of Athanasius, and to concoct a new series of charges against his honour and loyalty.

Ursacius and Valens recanted their recantation of Arian doctrine and strategy. On the advance of Constantius through Italy in the contest with Magnentius, he found the Western bishops in communion and in communication with Athanasius, and, 'like one

---

[1] This letter occurs in two forms—in the *Apologium ad Constantium*, § 23, and *Arian History*, § 24; in both cases avowed translations from Latin into Greek

set on fire, suddenly changed his mind, and no longer remembered his oaths, but was alike forgetful of what he had written and regardless of the duty he owed his brother.'[1] At Arles and Milan, he furiously attacked all who sympathized with the great Alexandrine bishop,—sent letters to the prefect of Alexandria, to take the corn revenues for the poor from Athanasius and give them to the Arians. Numerous steps were adopted to humiliate the chief pastor in the presence of his flock.

Still the storm had not broken over him. Other enemies of the Arian faith had felt the bitterness of the revenge. So early as the year of the return of Athanasius, at the first Council of Sirmium, 347, Photinus, the disciple of Marcellus, had been condemned; and after the decisive battle of Mursa, in the year 351-2, a second synod was held at Sirmium, where teacher and disciple were again condemned, and Basil was sent to Ancyra in place of Marcellus, but Athanasius was allowed to remain in his see. The plot was not ripe. Nor was the time wasted by the indefatigable defender of the faith, for he wrote at this period: (1) His work *Concerning the Opinions of Dionysius*, his illustrious predecessor at Alexandria. (2) His *Apology against the Arians*, called also *Syllogus*, a collection of historical documents, on which he rested his own vindication. (3) His treatise entitled *The Nicene Definition of the Faith*, in which he emphasized the supreme act of God's creation as distinct from all the secondary creations of men effected out of pre-existing material, and also contrasts Divine generation of the Son with human generation (§ ii.). He anticipated in this treatise much subsequently stated in the *Discourses against the*

[1] *Arian History*, § 30.

Arians, and vindicated the Nicene definition by references to Dionysius and Origen.

Julius, the Bishop of Rome, died in April, 352, and his see was, in May, conferred on the notorious Liberius. The semi-Arian party immediately plied the new Bishop of Rome with cruel accusations against Athanasius; but Liberius did not swerve from the course taken by his predecessor. Hosius of Cordova, Paulinus of Trèves, were also faithful to the doctrine, and ready to defend the honour of Athanasius.

Meanwhile the mind of the Emperor was becoming more and more poisoned against Athanasius; and the beginning of the great breach was effected by the effort that the latter made to avert it. He sent envoys from Alexandria to the Emperor, who was then residing at Milan in the year 353. The embassage consisted of five bishops (Serapion of Thmuis being one of them), and three presbyters, who were to bring facts before the mind of Constantius calculated to prove that this assault upon the character of the Bishop of Alexandria was simply another device for assailing and extinguishing the Nicene faith.

Before the envoy could have reached Milan a messenger arrived at Alexandria, bringing letters from the Emperor, which implied that Athanasius had requested an interview with him, and stated that this request was complied with, and summoning the bishop to the court. Now Athanasius had written no such letter, and the summons appeared to all his friends at Alexandria to be a mere decoy to put him physically in the toils of his malignant enemies. Athanasius saw through the device; and while he declared that he 'was not so mad as to refuse an order from his majesty,' yet, seeing he had made no such request as that which was stated, he should venture to remain where he was until the command reached him. The Arian party around Constantius declared that such recusancy was high treason, and still further embittered the mind of the Emperor against their victim. Athanasius declared in his *Apology to Constantius* that twenty-six months elapsed before he received any communication from the court, and that throughout he had acted on the authority of the letters on the merits of which he had returned to Alexandria in 347, and that he was acting on the suggestions and promises contained in the imperial letters of 350, written immediately after the death of Constans.

Meanwhile Liberius had requested the Emperor to call a council to investigate the charges persistently brought against Athanasius; and the Arians had prevailed upon him to gather such a synod around him at Arles in 353. The delegates sent by the pope were Bishops Vincent of Capua and Marcellus of Campania, who unfortunately, with the view of gaining time, declared that they would sign the condemnation of Athanasius, if the hostile party would pronounce anathemas upon the Arian heresy. At first this injudicious scheme seemed to succeed, but it soon appeared that those time-serving turncoats, Ursacius and Valens, and the rest of the party would pronounce no such anathemas upon Arian doctrine, and yet fiercely demanded the deposition of Athanasius. It was disastrous, and to the cruel chagrin of Liberius, that the Roman delegates succumbed to the vehement pressure of the court, of the Empress Eusebia, of the majority of the council, and to the threats of Constantius. Paulinus of Trèves was the only Athanasian prelate who stood firm, and he was banished to Phrygia, and bereft there of all companionship but that of the Montanists.

Still, no positive step was taken to carry this condemnation into effect. Liberius condemned and grieved over his own legates. Lucifer of Cagliari raged, fumed, and poured forth torrents of indignation against the Arians and the Emperor; demanded for the Church its utter independence of the secular power, and in language as bitter as that adopted by the wildest *circumcelliones* of Africa.

Athanasius was accused of all kinds of inconsistent actions and principles; *e.g.*, Constantius was persuaded to believe that during the civil and bloody war with the usurper Magnentius, and even before the death of Constans, Athanasius had temporized with Magnentius. The *Apology to Constantius* contains a noble, pathetic and courageous rejoinder, revealing the hollowness, insincerity and contradictory character of the charge. How could he have approved the hostile attitude of a practical heathen and treacherous barbarian towards his best political friend?

Meanwhile other events were occurring big with the destinies of the future. Constantius had summoned Julian, his nephew—the pupil of Eusebius of Nicomedia, the enthusiastic student of philosophy, the secret worshipper of the ancient gods—from the University of Athens to the tented field. He had invested him with the purple and the title of Cæsar, and bidden him drive the northern barbarians from Gaul. He may have wished to extinguish him. There was no love lost between uncle and nephew. They hated one another with deadly scorn. Constantius was in a measure a theologian, who with passionate partisanship espoused a side in the mighty intellectual contest concerning the nature of the Godhead, and yet he was much mystified by the intensity with which the rival parties disputed the profound metaphysics of the question. He was fully alive, however, to the enormous moral and social force which issued from the teaching of Athanasius, and felt instinctively that that teaching undermined his own authority and tended to destroy his influence

Julian looked at the entire controversy with humorous and yet indignant disgust, and would have consorted with Athanasius or Ursacius, Lucifer or Leontius, on equal terms. Nothing pleased him better than to set the rivals by the ears, and he was diverted by their, to him, unmeaning wrangle. By some strange evolution, a dormant faculty of military and political strategy was suddenly developed in Julian, and he achieved extraordinary successes in Gaul, and became the idol of the army and a new terror for the mean soul of Constantius.

While Julian was fighting the Allemanni, the Arian bishops were condemning and sending to exile Lucifer of Cagliari, Eusebius of Vercelli, and Dionysius of Milan, for their refusal either to communicate with them or to condemn Athanasius. These holy men were led in chains, as common criminals, to their various places of exile, and 'as they passed along they preached the Gospel in every place and city, proclaiming the orthodox faith and anathematizing the Arian heresy.'[1]

Athanasius was in the thick of the great battle with a world which seemed to have become Arianized under his very eyes. Yet there are scenes and affairs of pathetic interest disclosed. One of his writings *(Epistola ad Dracontium)* reveals him in a new character. A young presbyter, the abbot of a neighbouring monastery, much beloved by his monks, devoted with enthusiasm to the solitary life, was regarded by

[1] *Arian History*, § 34

Athanasius as a highly suitable man to become a bishop. He had been elected by a small diocese to the office in a transport of enthusiasm. Athanasius was charmed by the thought of finding in him a colleague and participator in his conflict with evil and error. He sought, and even hastened, to consecrate him; but the young man shrunk from the charge, pleaded his youth and inexperience, an impediment in his speech, a feeble voice, and the temptations which habitually waited on all public ministration of the Word. His monks inspired these unworthy fears; but the sage counsels of the persecuted patriarch prevailed, and Dracontius was made bishop.

Dracontius had hardly commenced his duties when in sheer confusion and distress, like Chrysostom, Fulgentius and others, he fled once more into the depths of the desert. The letter which Athanasius wrote to him casts a most gracious side-light on the fatherly, faithful, devout and spiritual side of the great theological disputant. Athanasius pleaded most tenderly with his young friend, described his own grief, just as the father of the prodigal son might have done. He trembled over the perilous effect produced upon the Church and on unconverted heathen by such dereliction of duty. He urged that a man may be saved while pursuing the practical secular work of the clergy as well as in the depths of the cloister or the cave, and declared that in his case there would be more commendable sacrifice of self in fulfilling the duties to which he had been summoned than in the soul-saving austerities of the monastic life. Let him be conscious of weakness of voice and nerve, had not Moses made the same complaint? Did not Jeremiah intercede with God that he too was a child? Did not Jonah tremble and flee to his own discomfiture from the first summons to active service ? Let Dracontius trust in God, and leave the issue of life or death, of persecution or peace, to the blessed Lord Himself.

We do not know for certain the result, for troublous times were at hand. But there is reason to believe that during Constantius' vehement persecution of the Nicene party in the year 356, Dracontius suffered, but not unto death, since he seems to have been present as a bishop at the Council of Alexandria in 362. His name also was fragrant in the deserts of Nitria and elsewhere.[1]

Thus a gleam of light on one little glade of a widespreading shadowy forest of great deeds reveals the beauty of the wild flowers and tender greens and busy life that may be adorning the depth of the untrodden woods, on which no such illuminating beam has glanced

Having secured banishment and deposition for the illustrious Paulinus and Dionysius and Eusebius of Vercelli, the Arian party pursued their advantage, and plotted to break in pieces the unanimous support hitherto granted to Athanasius by the Western Church. In the year 355 they contrived to secure a large gathering of bishops at Milan under the sanction of Constantius. The entire proceedings were clamorous and indecent in the extreme. By threats of physical force, by cruel sarcasms, by party manœuvres, they effected a widespread defection in the number of the friends of Athanasius. Hilary of Poictiers, one who late in life was forced to take up the controversy, whose mastery of the whole subject was highly appreciated, and whose acceptance of the Nicene faith was achieved by personal and ardent study of

---

[1] See Tillemont, *Memoires. Saint Athanase*, art. lxvii.

Holy Scripture, was forced to make his appearance either at Arles or Milan, and there confronted with some trumped-up charge against his moral character, which in 356 was regarded as sufficient to secure his banishment. Public notaries were sent in all directions to command the bishops and people to believe in the accusations asserted, but never investigated and proved against Athanasius, to refuse all communion with him, and to accept on the other hand the fellowship of his malignant enemies.

There were two distinguished ecclesiastics whom as yet the Arians were not able to bend or coerce: Hosius of Cordova had watched over the great controversy from its beginning, and took a leading part in the Council of Nicæa thirty years before. The snows of nearly a hundred years had descended upon him. His wisdom, his dignity, his enormous influence overshadowed that of Athanasius, or even that of the Roman pontiff. The party of the Emperor and his Arian advisers planned to break the last plank which survived between the see of Alexandria and the dominant Church, and for the purpose of destroying Athanasius they resolved to drag the hoary hair of Hosius in the dust, and also to break the hitherto indomitable will of Liberius. The Emperor sent a special envoy with presents to the pope, demanding from him assent to the condemnation of Athanasius. Liberius boldly and nobly declined to grant it, on the ground that the charges had been refuted by the great Council of Sardica. He demanded in return that another free council should be held, *at a distance from the court,* for a full investigation of every charge. Doctrine must be understood first; and when we know by this test the parties to whom this decision can be entrusted, then let the investigation proceed. The presents sent by the Emperor were unceremoniously rejected, and the entire conduct of the pope was so uncompromising that Constantius compelled him to come to his presence. Here, though Liberius was as outspoken and determined as ever, the Emperor took no heed of his remonstrance, and banished him to Berœa, in Thrace. He proudly refused to receive presents of money, which were sent him from the Emperor, Empress, and court.[1]

But so long as Hosius of Cordova stood erect the fury of the Arians was not slaked. They contrived to subpœna the old man from Spain to Milan. On arrival he was commanded, as Liberius had been, to renounce the convictions of his lifetime. For a while the profound impression of his personal presence and the unanswerable arguments of his grand letter to Constantius prevailed.[2] This letter is one of the most noticeable and interesting of the whole series. In it Hosius shows how confident he was of the innocence of Athanasius, maintains that the Church could not and would not receive its doctrine from the State, recounts the scandalous proceedings of the Arians at Sardica, the recantations of Ursacius and Valens, the previous conduct of Constantius himself, his promises, letters and orders; and he concludes thus: 'Cease then, I beseech you, O Constantius, and be persuaded by me. These things it becomes me to write, and you not to despise.' Notwithstanding this, Hosius was brutally summoned again from Cordova to Sirmium in 355, and there kept in virtual durance for twelve months, where, by dint of incessant persecution and cruel confinement, and when broken by suffering and

[1] Theodoret (*H E*, ii 16) gives a vivid account of this scene.
[2] *Arian History*, § 44.

extreme age, he was forced rather than persuaded, two
years later, after the impending blow had fallen upon
Athanasius, to hold communion with Ursacius, but
would never be persuaded to condemn Athanasius, and
at the approach of death anathematized the Arian
doctrine.

Another interesting event preceded the final *coup
d'état* by which the deposition of Athanasius was at
last effected. The churches in Alexandria were
numerous, but insufficient to accommodate the vast
crowds who gathered for worship. Nine of these
churches were enumerated by Epiphanius, and among
them were those dedicated to St. Dionysius and St.
Theonas. But there was a vast enclosure, called the
Cæsareum, near the palace, which Gregory, the in-
truded bishop, had begun, under the suggestion and
at the expense of Constantius, to transform into a
church of great size. It bore the name of the Emperor.
Gregory never completed his task; but after the
return from his second exile in 347, Athanasius quietly
resumed the undertaking, and though the building
was not consecrated in 355, it was ready for use.

The multitudes who filled the churches for prayer
and ordinances were so vast that frequent accidents
occurred. Old men and maidens had been crushed in
the crowds, and carried away more dead than alive. In
view of the approaching Easter ceremonies, Athanasius
yielded, after urgent pressure and some remonstrance,
to the intense desire of the people to celebrate the
great festival in the Cæsareum. In his *Apology to
Constantius* (§ 17) he vindicated his conduct in noble
words, and on grounds of strong common sense and
spiritual insight. Yet even this act was brought
against Athanasius by his Arian enemies, who represented it as contrary to rule and disrespectful to the

Emperor. This charge shows that the Arian party, as a whole, were becoming formalists in their rubric as well as unscrupulous in their tactics. Athanasius, in almost playful manner, puts the matter before Constantius (*see* §§ 17, 21), and imagines the vituperative use that would have been made of his own conduct if he had despised the building that was being erected in the city by command of the Emperor, and had led out the multitudes beyond the walls to pray in the wilderness.

Before this celebrated *Apology* was written the blow fell upon the African Church and upon the great archbishop. An imperial notary, Diogenes by name, at length arrived in July or August, 355, and made Athanasius understand that he must soon be dislodged. This Diogenes endeavoured first to sow dissension and excite fear among the clergy of the city. They, however, demanded a sight of the written orders of the Emperor, which the envoy could not produce. The people armed themselves to defend their chief pastor from all forcible arrest or capture, and this symptom of enthusiasm and violent passion led the imperial officer to congregate the legions of the army already stationed in Libya and Egypt.

At the beginning of the following year, 356, Syrianus, *dux Egypti*, siding with Diogenes, made a bold effort to force Athanasius to leave his seat and abdicate his functions, and that at the suggestion and command of the Emperor. But Duke Syrianus, Maximus the Prefect, and others who urged the claim, were so far impressed with the equity of Athanasius' contention that they admitted the right to hold his position so long as the letters sent to him by Constantius in 350 had not been cancelled by the imperial sign-manual. Athanasius told Constantius

afterwards that he did feel suspicious of the straight-
forwardness or reality of the mission of Diogenes and
of the orders received by Syrianus. At length the
pledge was given with a great oath that the written
authority of the Emperor should be produced before
any steps were taken by them. The vast Christian
population was quieted and reduced to false security;
all the people assembled together in the churches with
feelings of joyfulness. But three and twenty days
after, long before the authorization of Constantius
could have arrived, or even a demand for it reach him,
the blow was struck. Constantius—like Philip of
Spain and Charles I. of England, and other wily,
despotic natures—often devised that steps should be
taken which he eagerly desired, but which at the time
it was his policy personally to disavow. His representatives had no direct authority to apprehend
Athanasius, but they ventured to act (as Caiaphas
and Annas had on a similar occasion dared to do) in
the dead of night, when Athanasius had gathered a
congregation at the Church of St. Theonas, and was
conducting a vigil in anticipation of the communion
on the following day. While the people were softly
chanting the Psalms, the military authorities proceeded
in cruel and bloodthirsty fashion to perpetrate their
stealthy and wicked deed. Syrianus surrounded the
church with five or six thousand armed men, and
burst into the building, spreading round the congregation with drawn swords, bows, spears and clubs,
and enclosing it as in a net. Athanasius[1] describes
the scene with his own pen: 'I considered it would
be unfair in me to desert the people during such
a disturbance; therefore I sat down upon my throne,

---

[1] *Apol. pro Fuga*, § 34.

ESCAPE INTO THE WILDERNESS.

and desired the deacon to read the Psalm cxxxvi., and the people to answer, *for His mercy endureth for ever*, and then all to depart.'

The Arian party, like Judas of old, were there to guide the Roman soldiers to their victim; but amid the gradual disappearance of the people and clergy, not only did the monks, presbyters and deacons, in some mysterious fashion vanish in the dim light and crossing shadows, but the great bishop vanished too from the eager searchers who would have destroyed or kidnapped him. The scene is sublime and weird— the scent of these bloodhounds failed them. It is true that many of the poor folk were mortally injured in the *mêlée*, virgins were maltreated and slain; but while the deacon read, ' To Him that smote Egypt in their firstborn,' . . . 'and brought out Israel from among them,' 'with a strong hand and with a stretched-out arm,' . . . 'and to Him who led His people through the wilderness'; and while the congregation thundered forth in the tumult between each strophe, 'for His mercy endureth for ever,' God covered Athanasius with the shadow of His hand, and so he passed through the midst of his enemies into the depth of the wilderness. Where he was concealed none knew. Constantius used every effort to find him, but failed; yet from the profound secret of his hiding-places he sent forth Apologies, Encyclicals, Discourses, Comments, and Epistles which shook the world.

CHAPTER X.

THE MINISTRY OF THE WILDERNESS.

WE cannot determine where Athanasius lay hidden from the sight of his persistent enemies. According to one improbable account,[1] he was shielded from all pursuit in the house of a virgin of Alexandria, a lady gifted with phenomenal beauty, who poured water on his feet, supplied him with the necessaries of life, and provided him with books and information during a space of six years. Some truth may lie in the story. It is not improbable that after the tragic scene in the church of St. Theonas he was protected by some such device from the fierce search of Arian and Pagan foes; but the numerous efforts made by them under the instigation of Constantius, and spurred on by his violent letters to the Alexandrian people, and even to the farfamed Bishop Frumentius, at Auxume (see p. 41), make it extremely unlikely that he could have been concealed during this long and eventful period in the suburbs of Alexandria, though he may have occasionally visited his flock under some deep disguise. According to one account, based on a doubtful sentence in the *Epistle of Athanasius concerning the Councils of Ariminum and Seleucia* (§ 1), he was even an unrecognised visitor or assessor at the Council of Seleucia. But most probably he was hidden in some of the numberless caves and cells of the monks of Scetis and of the Nitrian desert, and occasionally hurried from one to another in the dead of night. Intensely ascetic, spare, lithe, agile and wary, endowed with enormous

[1] Sozomen, *H E*, v. 6.

courage and dauntless will, he was able by these rapid movements to baffle the eager search of his malicious enemies, who, wherever they went after him, even to the borders of Abyssinia, found his name and prestige mightier than the armies, the spies, and the sonorous titles of Constantius, Cæsar, Maximus, Victor, Augustus.

For a while Athanasius cherished the hope that Constantius would disown the virulent and shameful maltreatment of his flock, and that he might be able to explain to the Emperor in person the infamous machinations of the Arians; and even in his *Apology to Constantius* he still gives the Emperor personal credit for benignity towards himself, speaking of his 'piety' and 'godliness,' recounting his own entire loyalty to the supreme throne, and confessing himself shocked by, and disdainful of the charges brought against his honour. In other and later works, he adopted, after much bitter experience, another tone, compared Constantius with the worst of Christ's persecutors, and even suggested that he is none other than 'the Antichrist' of prophecy.

Athanasius had reason for his change of tone. One disaster after another fell upon his lacerated, tortured spirit. Soon after he had been forced into this mysterious exile he must have heard of the treatment to which Hosius of Cordova, Liberius of Rome, and Marcellus, his old friend, had been again subjected for remaining faithful to himself, and how for a while they too, in the stress of great temptation, yielded apparently to the storm, and even signed Arian formulæ.

One grievous weapon used was a persistent attempt to blacken his character, even with his own people, accusing him to them of the sin of cowardice, for 'the flight' which, notwithstanding all their mean intrigue and desperate effort, they could not track. His *Apology for Flight* is a noble vindication of his position. He justified his conduct by Christ's own words, and by the example of the Lord Himself on several well-known occasions. He urged the precedent of St. Peter and St. Paul when they were distressed by analogous circumstances; he quoted the Christian injunction to flee from the persecutor, if by such means an apostle might the better serve the Church. In noble words he recounted the flight of Moses, and showed how it was compatible with heroism and courage. He recalls how Elijah, who had hidden himself from Jezebel, was willing to confront Ahab, and maintains that St. Paul's departure from Damascus and from Jerusalem harmonizes with his martyr-like courage in his Roman dungeon.

This apology was written between the lapse of Hosius and that of Liberius, about the end of 357; and in it he distinctly repudiates the legitimacy of persecution. 'If it be a bad thing to flee, it is much worse to persecute; for the one party hides himself to escape death, the other persecutes with desire to kill.' He adds: 'Persecution is a device of the devil, and one which he seeks to exercise against all.' Augustine, in his letter ccxxviii., elaborately deals with the question of flight under such circumstances, when the servant of God is fleeing from a personal search made after himself, and he largely justifies 'the holy Athanasius.'

The closing words of the *Apology to Constantius* are full of fiery disdain of these tactics, and a great hope for happier days. But these days were not yet.

(1) *The Fate of the Church in Egypt.*

The Emperor not only pursued Athanasius with

virulent hatred, and heaped upon him the most opprobrious epithets, such as 'villain,' 'pestilent fellow,'[1] but allowed deeds much worse than words to be done in Egypt by the forcible intrusion of George of Cappadocia into the see of Alexandria. George was so extreme an Arian as to make himself utterly obnoxious to the semi-Arian party. He adopted the Anomæan hypothesis, which was to the effect that the nature of the Son was *unlike* the nature of the Father. He was of low origin and bad habits, turbulent, violent, cruel, tyrannous, and, according to Athanasius, no Christian in any sense. The letters of Julian and the history of Sozomen show that he could hardly have been the uneducated man suggested by some, as he was possessed of a library of great extent and value. He secured the favour of Constantius and was extolled by the Emperor as a man of learning, sanctity and wisdom.

The Egyptian churches and bishops generally were violently threatened and cruelly forced to enter into communion with George and to renounce the crimes and venomous follies of Athanasius. Scenes were again enacted as bloodthirsty and truculent as those which had occurred during the intrusive episcopate of Gregory. Virgins were stripped, exposed, and beaten; bishops were led away in chains; congregations which had assembled in secluded places for worship were, like the Covenanters of later days, broken up by violence; private houses were pillaged. The bread of widows and orphans was snatched from their feeble hands; tombs were rifled of their occupants, lest peradventure Athanasius were concealed amid the

[1] These and like terms occur in the letters of Constantius to the Alexandrians, etc., preserved in the *Apology to Constantius*, §§ 29, 30, which Athanasius politely assumes then as of doubtful authenticity.

mummied corpses; many monasteries were destroyed, and the 'religious' were threatened with fiery death. The name of the Emperor was ever on the lips of the persecutors, whose lines of action were directed and abetted by Count Heraclius, by the Dux Sebastian (said to be a Manichee), and the Prefect Cataphronius. The Arian youth were encouraged to tear the veils from the faces of virgins whom they met in the streets, but who would not compromise their faith. Eutychus the deacon was beaten with violence, and then condemned to exile in a distant inhospitable desert. He died on the way to his destination, rejoicing in the crown of a veritable martyrdom for the Divinity of his Lord. The Arians were put in possession of the churches.

All this occurred at Whitsuntide; but a week later, on June 2nd, the like cruelties were again and again enacted. Throughout the province of Athanasius his suffragan bishops were ruthlessly torn from their flocks, sent to the quarries, loaded with chains, and threatened with the punishment of treason. Some yielded to the terrible pressure, but more than 90 (according to Athanasius, in his *Letters to the Libyan and Egyptian Bishops*) suffered intolerable hardship. Some were old men who had been consecrated by Peter the Martyr and Alexander, others were sick unto death; but George and his instruments had no mercy. Among these sufferers were Dracontius (see p. 82), Serapion of Thmuis, Ammonius, Philo, Thenas, Adelphius, and Presbyters Hierax, and Dioscurus, and many others of less renown.

The cruelties of George were not limited to the orthodox Christians; 'towards all alike (says Sozomen *H. E.*, iv. 10, 30) he acted so as to strike terror, and wielded his authority with violence.' He was hated

by the magistrates and the people ; and, avaricious in
the extreme, he made cruel requisitions on his flock.
He used violent means to crush the pagan super-
stitions. We must not forget that the temple of
Serapis was still one of the wonders of the world,
glittering with all the pomp of both Greek and
Egyptian idolatry ; and, more for the sake of plunder
than for the overthrow of paganism, he committed the
grossest sacrilege on this superb monument of the
ancient faith, to which perhaps a third of the city
still adhered. In the spring of 358 he began to reap
the reward of his tyranny and fanaticism.

(2) *The Writings of Athanasius during this Exile.*

Meanwhile the 'invisible patriarch' was incessantly
occupied. Dwelling in the humble mud-huts of the
tiny villages, or hiding in the cells and tombs which
honeycombed the rocks of the Thebaid or Libyan
desert, with 'runners' ready at peril of life to convey
his missives to bishops and monasteries, he must have
been perpetually active, writing his famous *Arian
History*, a portion only of which has been preserved; his *Encyclical Epistle to the Egyptian and
Libyan Bishops against the Arians* (some have supposed this to have been written in 356, after *the*
return from his second exile, but the indications of
time are faint and few) ; his *Apology to Constantius*,
his *Letter to Serapion anent the Death of Arius; the
Apology for his Flight;* but, above all, his celebrated
Four Discourses against the Arians.

Much of his time was doubtless spent in the
society of the anchorites whom he loved so well,
and in the practice of their simple duties and sweet
reconcilement. His ascetic and self-mortifying habits,

his readiness to share the humblest avocations, and by fasting and prayer to place himself at their side and share their lot, excited their boundless enthusiasm, coupled, as the sight of his outward demeanour must have been, with their reflection that he was throughout the veritable patriarch of one of the most dignified sees in the Christian Church. According to Gregory of Nazianzus, the persecutors, when they fancied themselves on the whereabouts of the illustrious exile, could never extract a solitary word from any of the recluses of the desert, who bowed their necks for the sword, but refused to utter a sound, lest they should betray him, believing that in suffering death for Athanasius they were simply serving the Lord Jesus Christ.

The fascination which this extraordinary man exercised over those who knew and loved him was one of the romantic features of his immense personality. In the *Life of Pachomius* we are told that Duke Artemius, who was pursuing the search, asked the leader of a monastic settlement, 'Is Athanasius here?' and received for answer, 'He is indeed the father of us all, but I have never seen his face.' The danger Athanasius felt that he was bringing upon his friends induced him to penetrate deeper and deeper into the desert, until one solitary female for some time watched over his strange hiding-place. He lay concealed (says Sozomen, *H. E.*, iv. 10) in a dry cistern, from which, on the approach of danger, he escaped. Whether true or not, it is a hint of his manner of life from 356-361.

We may fancy him sitting in the shadow of the portico of a tomb, penning with *stylus* on piles of papyrus the documents which preserve so much of his life, recounting his relations with the great saints

AN EGYPTIAN VILLAGE.

and statesmen of his troubled days, and recording his profoundest thoughts touching the deep mystery of the Godhead.

(3) *The Four Discourses against the Arians.*

This is a convenient place for exhibiting the general character of his greatest work, *The Four Discourses against the Arians.*[1] These celebrated discussions—at least three of them—form one connected argument, and one continuous controversial handling of the chief doctrinal positions and negations of the Arians. They are also a vindication of the true sense of Scripture against the perverted use of it by the Arian writers. Consequently the discourses are Biblical rather than scholastic in their form. Athanasius endeavoured to put the genuine revelation of God in Holy Scripture before his readers, rather than the decision of Nicæa, or of any earlier or later council. He took for granted that all Christians did hold, or ought to have held, as supremely fundamental, the unity or the solity of God, and the existence of the Son of God. The reverence of Christians towards the Christ, who was believed to be the Word and Wisdom of God made flesh, had for hundreds of years led them to heap upon His holy name every term of honour, worship, and renown which human lips could frame.

---

[1] Modern students have easy access to Dr. Bright's excellent preface to his edition of the Greek text, to Cardinal Newman's translation, in 2 vols., of *The Library of the Fathers*, to Bishop Kaye's *Council of Nicæa*, etc., where the reader will find a careful analysis. See also Tillemont and Ceillier for valuable digests.

But the question which had become of burning interest and transcendent importance was, 'Is the Son of God veritable God or not?' If He be *not* true God, then we have (said Athanasius) *two* Gods, for He is by His nature, as well as by His incarnation, the express image, revelation, word, and wisdom of the Father. If He *be* true God, said the Arians, then the distinction between the Father and Son vanishes, and all the outcome and forth-putting of His glory is a partitive, physical break-up of the Divine essence. Arius, Eusebius of Nicomedia, Asterius, and all the elder Arians charged the orthodox party with repeating the error of Sabellius, while the Athanasian party regarded every tendency towards Arianism as a movement in direction of ditheism and polytheism.

The reader of these famous discourses is struck by the entire or almost complete silence of their author over the catch-words of the two great parties. He does not press the word HOMOOUSION, nor refer to the Homoiousion of the semi-Arians, or the *Anomoion* of Eunomius, Aetius, and George; nor does he at this time show intimate acquaintance with the Homæan party or leaders, but he rejects and dismisses the ideas connoted by these phrases as ruinous to Christian teaching, as dishonouring to God, as cruel to the souls of men.

The extreme ultra-Arianism of George, who had been thrust into his own episcopate of Alexandria, may perhaps account for the eagerness with which Athanasius handles here the old Arian formulæ which he had confronted nearly thirty years before, instead of the delicate subtleties of the semi-Arians or the curious and bewildering eclecticism of the followers of Marcellus. The desert must have been once more resounding with the old war-cries. 'The Son was not before He was begotten,' 'There was [a period, a past eternity] . . . when He was not.' The hard, dogmatic Arianism, with its stereotyped and unscriptural phrases, had been revived in North Africa by the followers of George and by the favour of Constantius; and the venerable but invisible warrior was as ready as ever to unhorse these doughty and desperate champions of a rationalistic and unspiritual faith.

The form and phraseology of the attack is often too severe for modern refinement of manners. Arians were charged with 'venom' and 'viperous spirit,' they were 'insensate,' 'impious,' even 'atheistic' in their views, 'maniacal,' 'God-hating,' 'God-fighting,' 'Christ-fighting' fanatics (*Theomachoi* and *Christomachoi*). However, allowance must be made for the rhetoric that was adopted in those days, and notice be taken of the cruel tactics and strategy which we have already described, which must have tended to confound, even in the mind of this great thinker, Arian opinion with the malignity of their ecclesiastical rivalry, their religious ideas with the secularism and duplicity of their practical aims.

The first discourse seems tolerably complete in itself; and it is probable that copies of it fell into the hands of his enemies, seeing that the second discourse refers to some of the comments made by Arians upon the first. The fourth discourse, in the opinion of many competent writers, looks rather like the disconnected notes and headings of a treatise which had not been thoroughly digested. We imagine that the whole, before it was finally issued from the copyists, must have suffered careful editing from the author.

The commencement of the treatise savours too much of violent abuse. A handle is made of the circumstance that his opponents had adopted the *name* 'Arian,' thereby relinquishing, after the manner of earlier heretics, the title of Christian altogether, in favour of the teacher who led them astray. 'The earlier disciples' (said he) 'did not call themselves by the name of the Apostles. All were called by the one name on whom they placed their faith.' This remark is interesting to-day, when so much is made in some schools of New Testament criticism of the supposed rivalries between the Pauline and Petrine parties in the early Church. Athanasius had no tradition of them!

The main strain of the argument turns upon the identity of the terms, 'Son,' 'Word,' 'Wisdom,' 'Image,' 'Power,' 'Hand,' of the Father. Each term may emphasize some one quality or function of one and the same unchangeable Hypostasis (*ousia*, or *substantia*) of the Father; but they each, separately and all combined, and all in one, appertain to the essence of God. He does not use the Nicene term, '*homóousios* with the Father,' but labours to show that the Father is not, and never could have been, *God,* if He had been without *Logos* (ἄλογος), or without 'word,' wisdom, or power; that the effluence of the 'light' is co-eternal with the Light; that from eternity He must have sustained the relation of Father to Son actually, not by mere anticipation. We cannot worship a creature, however exalted above all other creatures. To call 'a creature' God is a misnomer, and is a peril to the religious faculty. Such conduct either falls back into paganism or borders on atheism.

Athanasius is aware that the Arians regarded the Logos who was 'with God and was God,' as distinct from the Logos which was incarnate; that they held that the Eternal Wisdom *generated* the Son of God, and that our Lord was only by courtesy called Wisdom and Word, because He became a partaker in such wisdom (I. § 9); and Athanasius does not think the speculation is worth a moment's consideration. A full answer to Arius would have necessitated an exposition of what was supposed to take place in the *incarnation.* He is satisfied with the unique elevation of nature which justified Christ in the utterance of such an expression as, 'I am the light,' and in accepting the declaration, 'Thou art My beloved Son.' Athanasius does not hesitate to affirm that 'the Eternal Power and Godhead' (Rom. 1. 20) *is* the Son of God (§ 12). He draws the conclusion that the Son of God is eternal and unoriginate from such expressions as 'I AM,' not, 'I was made' the light, the way, the life, the shepherd. It is only of created things of which a period previous to their existence is spoken, and the entire phraseology is 'alien to the Word.' To imagine 'times when He was not' is to blaspheme His majesty. Nothing but equivocation is involved in such a formula as 'There was, when He was not.' Arians *meant* a time or times, even if they pretended to leave out the idea of time.

The Arians replied that the very term 'sonship' would lose all meaning if it be supposed an *eternal* act or relationship. Brotherhood would be a more appropriate phrase. It is possible that the extreme position taken up by Eunomius, the Bishop of Cyzicus, and disciple of Aëtius, namely, the utter *unlikeness* between Father and Son, had been communicated to Athanasius in his exile, and that this view, which was regarded by the semi-Arians as blasphemy, was here treated as identified with the Arian theology. The reply (§ 14, etc.) is, that no hint whatever occurs that there is any antecedent principle ($ἀρχή$) from which the Father and Son could have alike proceeded. Human generation is in *time*, subject to chronology, but Divine generation is irrespective of time. God's generation, since He can *never* have lacked any element of perfection, was in eternity.

Once more we hear from Athanasius that God could never have been without His proper *word* and *wisdom;* that the light could never have been without shining, nor the Fountain of Eternal Being barren and dry.

'It is all one to say, God is entirely participated, and that He begets; and what does begetting signify but a Son?' The generation of the Son does not imply any division of God's substance. [The term 'son' must be retained in order to maintain the 'monarchia' and 'greatness' of the Father, and from the numberless assertions of Scripture; but it does not connote all that is involved in the imperfect generation of created beings, and does connote infinitely more.]

The argument proceeds further to establish the eternity of the Son from the eternity of the *threefold* relations. 'There is only one glory of the Holy Three.' The Christian Trinity is not a pagan evolution, [He may have been contemplating the oriental *Trimurti*, or the Neoplatonic Triad], but an eternal and unchangeable ONE. [This argument would, in our theology, be a *petitio principii*. The *doctrine* of the *Trinity* is an induction arising out of belief in the consubstantiality of the Father and the Son and the Spirit; but Athanasius is apparently establishing the *latter* by the *former*. The explanation is to be found in the common theoretical acceptance by both parties to this controversy of the *unity* of the undivided Trinity. Such unity, Athanasius reasons, could not have been made up of dissimilars.]

A further argument is based (in § 20) on the Biblical idea that Christ is the *image* of the invisible God, the brightness of His glory and *express image* of His substance (Heb. i. 3). Granting the subsistence, there was forthwith its expression and image, not a something objective to itself, not a detached imitation, but of and in its essence. The 'form of God' must be eternal as God Himself.

It is noticeable that Athanasius, in this place particularly, avoids the use of the word *homoousios*. Is it conceivable that he was aware of how the contending Eunomians and semi-Arians were trying at the time when he penned this treatise to create a new formula of reconciliation, by ignoring the catchwords of the stormy controversy? (See pp. 93, 117.) In this perfect image and form of Himself, the Father, seeing Himself, has delight. When was the Father without this infinite joy? All the greatest and most essential attributes of the Father must be in the Son, that it may be true that whoso seeth the Son seeth the Father also. How could there be a likeness of Him who brought all things into being in what is itself produced out of nothing?

A very subtle objection is then cited. 'How is it, if the Son is *like in all things* to the Father—[a phrase which by the way was used a little later as an equivalent term to the *homoousion*, seeing that 'all things' ($\pi\acute{a}\nu\tau a$) must necessarily include 'substance']—He is not like Him in respect of generation also, and as He was begotten, was He not bound also to beget in His likeness, so that there would be an infinite series of fathers and sons? Athanasius says in reply, that this is another instance of arguing from imperfect analogies; and the absurdity of it is seen in carrying it a step further, and saying that the Father on the same understanding must be supposed to have a Father, and thus an infinite series in the past as well as the future would be involved.

To Athanasius, generation, like creation, was absolute, only complete and perfect in the case of 'the Father' and 'the Son.' 'The perfect nativity,' as Dr. J. H. Newman suggests, 'finds its termination in itself. The Son has not a Son because the Father has not a Father. "*The* Father" is the only true Father, and "*the* Son" the only true Son.'

The Arians suggested, that inasmuch as eternal creation is not necessary to constitute God from eternity as a Creator, so eternal generation, or the eternity of the Son, is not a necessary hypothesis for regarding the Father as an eternal Father, seeing that He may have been from eternity a Father *in posse*. Athanasius admits that creation in prospect is sufficient to constitute God an eternal Creator, because God is able to bring the non-existent into being out of nothing; but in the generation, the production is from Himself, from His eternal nature, and until He was actually a Father He cannot be thought of as such. Bishop Kaye condenses the argument well: 'God might be called Creator though nothing had been created; He had always the *power* to create; the non-existence of created things would be no diminution of His perfection. But He could not be called a Father unless He had a Son. If the Son did not always subsist with the Father, there would be a diminution of the perfection of the Father's essence.'

Athanasius here approaches the position of Augustine, that *Eternal Love* must needs have an eternal object of love, upon which to lavish the fulness of its being. The withdrawment from the concept of human generation, of so much that in current thought belongs to it, in order to set forth the Divine generation, and the constant recurrence to the analogous relation of God to His Word, His Wisdom, His Radiance, as qualities that are part of His essence, lifts the whole analogy of the sonship out of the horrible pit of biological speculation in which the Arian and Eunomian controversies were so prone to sink it.

We pass over the dispute concerning the two Greek words (ἀγένητος, ἀγέννητος), which Athanasius accuses the Arians with wilfully confounding, in order to bring the Son of God among the created things, and thus to deny His eternity. In § 35, he is roused to fiery earnestness by the specious argument that the Son of God is changeable, or, if not so, is destitute of freewill. First, he demonstrates the unchangeability of Him by whom we see and know the Father, and by which in reality we enter on the possession of the eternal life. He quotes Heb. xiii. 8; John xiv. 6; Psalm cii. 26; and in referring to the celebrated passage Phil. ii. 9, by which the Arians justified their contention, proceeded to show that their use of it involved a denial of the *pre-existence* of Christ altogether. This latter conclusion he refutes by numerous quotations from both the Old and New Testaments. Christ (says he) did not receive the title of Son and God as a reward. 'He was not man, and then became God, but He was God, and then became man, and that to make us gods' (§ 39). Moreover, the very passage on which he is commenting speaks of Christ as being in 'the form of God' before He was found in 'fashion as a man.'

The exaltation of which St. Paul speaks is a consequence of the Incarnation of the Word (John i. 1, 14). This great mystery expounds the other. 'God was humbled by taking our flesh; as man He underwent for us death in His flesh, that thereby He might offer Himself for us through death to the Father; therefore also as man He is said, because of us and for us, to be highly exalted, that as by His death we all died in

Christ, so again in the Christ Himself we might be highly exalted, being raised from the dead and ascending into heaven' (quoting Heb. vi. 20, and ix. 24). In a lengthened and eloquent passage, Athanasius sees in the exaltation of believers united to the Lord the full interpretation of St. Paul's words (see § 43).

He also further regards the exaltation of Christ from the grave as a direct consequence of His incarnation, because, as St. Paul argued elsewhere (1 Cor. xv.), He was 'the Man from heaven,' and 'the first to rise from the dead.' All other men had gone down into Hades, and were there still; but because Christ was originally and eternally in the form of God, *therefore* God exalted His humanity, and gave to His Divine-*human* Person the name above every name. The word '*given*' shows that it is not the Father that has become flesh, but it is His Word who has become man. What the Father gives, He, here as everywhere else, gives through His Son. Athanasius (as Dr. J. H. Newman has observed on this passage) is as explicit on the subject of the Divine-human Person, as if he had written after instead of before the Nestorian controversy.

Several sections follow in further vindication of the unchangeableness of the Son. An Arian argument was drawn from the Christian application of Psalm xlv. 5, 6, 'Thou art anointed with the oil of gladness above Thy fellows.' Athanasius (I. §§ 46, 47) urges that the oil of gladness with which the Christ was anointed above His fellows was no proof of the changeability of the Word, was no reward of the virtue of the *Word*,—whose throne as God was eternally the same,—but it was the exaltation of the *humanity*, which had been interpenetrated and baptized with the Spirit, and was now for ever lifted above all possibility of corruption or death.

He then proceeds with great fulness of illustration

to handle the Arian use of Heb. i. 1-4, and iii 2, which superficial readers might misapply. He is studious to show that Christ the Son is 'made better than the angels, *when* He had purged our sins,' and, therefore, in these last days of the Gospel Dispensation. He urges that the word 'better' proves that the whole nature of the Son incarnate and triumphant is superior in kind to that of the angels, as a son is better than a servant, and as the Occupant of the eternal throne is essentially superior to the ministering spirits. In a vast number of passages he endeavours to reveal the similar use of the term *better*, as adapted to express superiority in nature and essence, of which He is the sole participator, and not by a mere comparison 'better' in respect of things called into being by His Word.

He shows also that the uses of the word 'become' or 'made,' with reference to the offices of Christ, such as 'the surety of a better covenant,' are akin to those in which God Himself is made or becomes the Protector and Refuge of His people. Various texts in which the phrases 'He made' were applied to the mediatorial position of Christ, were used by Arians to demonstrate the created and entirely dependent position of the Son; but, as Athanasius says, 'It is inexcusable in them, because they might see that the expressions are to be understood of the appearance of Christ in the flesh.'

The same exegetical treatment of the Epistle to the Hebrews is continued in the *Second Discourse;* and he labours to show that the expression, 'was *faithful* to Him that made Him,' simply means '*trustworthy*' and faithful, *i.e.*, as God Himself is to all who put their confidence in Him. In this sense it is that He is a *faithful* High Priest. Moses was faithful as a servant,

Christ is faithful as a Son over His own house. 'He became faithful when He put on our flesh. Aaron was made high priest, being previously man, when he put on the robe of office; so our Lord the Word was made High Priest of our profession, when, though not changing His eternal essence, He put on our humanity for our sake, for the propitiation of our sins. His high priestly functions were accomplished by His Divine nature *in* and *according* to our humanity.

By this phraseology Athanasius seems to have steered His way between the two heretical speculations of the fifth century, which either in Nestorianism denied such union between His Divinity and humanity as practically to deny His Divinity, or in Apollinarianism and the later Monophysitism, virtually denied His humanity.

Similar lines of argument are followed through many sections in explanation of St. Peter's language in the Acts ii. 36 : 'He hath *made* Him both Lord and Christ.' This the Arians had wrested to their one-sided conclusion; but Athanasius shows it to mean that He who was the eternal Lord and King yet was made after the flesh, to redeem all, and to have dominion over all.

One of the Old Testament texts upon which the Arians enlarged was Proverbs viii. 22. This the LXX. translated, 'The Lord created me a beginning of His ways, with a view to His works.' Our A.V. and R.V. have translated it, 'The Lord possessed (or formed, *marg.*) me, in (or as) the beginning of His way before (or, the first of) His works of old.' So the Greek translator Aquila had translated the Hebrew word by ἐκτήσατο, rather than by ἔκτισε). Athanasius throughout abides by the reading of the LXX., but assigns to it the meaning of 'appointed.' He was, perhaps, induced to take this course from the frequent use of the same verb in Ecclesiasticus (i. 4, i. 9, and xxiv. 8), when the writer was portraying the dignity of 'Wisdom.' The Catholic expositors, like Jerome, preferred the other rendering, as there can be but little doubt that though *kana* (comp the Arab. form *kná*) has the root-idea of 'create,' yet it does not connote, like *bara*, the sense of commencement in time (Delitzsch: Comm. on the Proverbs, *in loco*). In *kanani* of Proverbs viii. 22 the idea is conveyed not only that Jehovah produced wisdom, but made Himself to possess it, not as something external to Himself, but as a bringing forth in it of His own creative efficiency.

At first Athanasius shows, by the whole teaching of other Scriptures, that Christ cannot be a creature, that He receives homage and worship from angels and apostles, which He could not have done if He had not been the proper offspring of the very essence of God. In this connection he uses the remarkable expression, that the *Son* of God is the very *Will* of God, by which all things were created, and urges from the natural correlation of God with His power, wisdom, word, image and radiance, that the laws of ordinary human thought refute the Arian gloss.

The wisdom of man is wrought in Him as type and image of the eternal wisdom. This type the Lord recognises in those who have received His Spirit, when, *e.g.*, identifying Himself with His disciples, He said, 'Saul, why persecutest thou ME?' So when the wisdom of God wrote, 'The Lord created me for His works,' this is not said of the wisdom which creates, but of its type created in His works.

It would be inappropriate here to follow the whole of the subtle argument by which Athanasius demonstrates with more of acuteness than force that the great passage in Proverbs viii. lends no support to the Arian doctrine.

The *third* discourse is divided into three parts, the first of which deals with the unity of the Father and Son; the second handles passages of Scripture which refer to the humanity of the Christ, but which had been used by the Arians to contest the Divinity of the Son; and the third is a reply to numerous objections.

The unity of the Father and the Son is maintained to be distinct altogether from the mutual indwelling of God and His saints, to rise above all material imagery whatever, to be unique. 'The whole being of the Son is proper to the Father's substance.' The form and Godhead of the Father is the Being of the Son, and so the Father is in the Son and the Son in the Father. In order to discriminate this from Sabellianism, he yet maintained with eagerness that the Father and Son are two, though the substance of the two is *one*.

The Arians urged that the Athanasian doctrine was incompatible with the prime truth of the unity of God, and involved a veritable tritheism; while Athanasius retorted that the Arians were open to the charge of polytheism, because 'they speak of the Son as a creature external to the Father, and that the Spirit *is* from that which is not'; that they were to be numbered with the Gentiles, inasmuch as they worshipped the creature (*see* iii. § 16).

Many sections are employed in the endeavour to point out the difference between the eternal mutual indwelling of the Father and the Son, and the derived perfection of the saints in their typical indwelling in the Father and Son. 'We dwell in Him (as St. John says 1 Ep. iv. 13) and He in us, because He has given us of His Spirit.' We are in Him by partaking of the Spirit. Now the Spirit is not that which constitutes the mutual indwelling, and on the contrary, the Spirit is given by the Son or is sent in His name.

We do not see why Athanasius should have hesitated to speak of the union of the Father and the Son as having been constituted from eternity in the consciousness of the Holy Spirit; and that the same Spirit is the unifying Energy, by which the Son of God and Son of man did indeed become one Christ, and also that by which the whole body of the faithful should be ultimately made perfect in One.

All the passages which speak of the lofty but subordinate dignities of the Son, and also of His limitations, sorrows and humiliations and Divine forsaking, are to be accounted for on the ground of the great underlying truth that God became flesh.

Nowhere do we find in the Nicene age a more emphatic expression of the redeeming work of Christ than in § 33, where he says 'If the works of the Godhead of the Word had not been done through the *body*, man would not have been deified ($\dot{\epsilon}\theta\epsilon o\pi o\iota\eta\theta\eta$) and if the things proper to the flesh had not been ascribed to the Word, man would not have been wholly delivered from them'; but the body itself is thus redeemed; 'men no longer remain sinners and dead according to their proper affections, but are raised up and remain for ever immortal and incorruptible. *Henceforward, our generation and every fleshly infirmity being transferred to the Word, we are raised from the earth, the curse through sin, being loosed through Him who is in us and becomes a curse for us.*'

One of the most difficult texts, and one which apparently sustains the Arian interpretation, is Mark

xiii. 32, where Christ admitted that 'the Son' as well as the angels was ignorant of the day and hour of His second coming. Athanasius, of course, does not refer this to the eternal Word, which was made flesh, but to the humanity with all its limitations and natural infirmities, and in respect of Christ's human ministry, of which this conscious ignorance was emphatically true.

This sympathy makes Him one with us. The Son of God and Lord of Glory in His humanity could feel hunger, thirst, even temptation to a self-centering use of the Divine energy, and could suffer, be crucified and die; and it is in perfect harmony with all this that He could voluntarily submit to the limitations of our knowledge, as well as to all the curse of our humanity.

Athanasius certainly approximates, in some passages, the admission that our Lord adopted an economical method of expression, saying that He *knew not* when as Son of God He undoubtedly did know, and was simply, *for the sake of* His disciples, withholding that which He actually had at His disposal for the advantage of His followers: he pursues the like argument with a multitude of further objections.

In the *fourth* discourse, we find rather the heads or draft of an argument which is not so much aimed against the Arians proper as against the opinions of many sectional developments of their views. The most interesting portion is that which has implicit reference to the later opinions of his eccentric and enthusiastic friend, Marcellus of Ancyra, to whom views had been attributed not far removed from Sabellianism. Athanasius does not mention him by name, but associates him with Photinus. The difficult question of the *time when* Athanasius refused reluctantly to sanction communion with Marcellus must here be passed by.

The interesting features of this entire series of discourses, forming as they do one of the most valuable of all the patristic writings, are their purely biblical character. Philosophical discourse, Platonic nomenclature, ecclesiastical definitions, conciliar adjudication of disputed questions, hardly appear throughout the discussion. The finest elements of modern exegesis reveal themselves. He is not content to take texts apart from their context, and give them a factitious sense due to doctrinal exigencies. He does not shirk difficulties, but appears doggedly to persist in an attempt to expound each great utterance with the utmost tenacity.

The language used by Athanasius is not always of the most courteous kind; but the great exile was a man, and it must not be forgotten that for twenty-six or even thirty years he had been the object of restless, reckless and malignant persecution; that while he wrote he was suffering cruel torture, defamation and misrepresentation for maintaining what he believed the Church had held from the beginning. He saw in Arianism the return to paganism, to polytheism, to subterfuge, and to a hopeless insufficiency of redemptive power for the salvation of the human soul,—and he was in no complimentary mood towards his adversaries.

The amazing knowledge and use of the canonical Scriptures which he displayed is a subsidiary argument of great potency for the place these sacred books had already taken in the judgment of Christian and Arian, Gnostic and unbeliever, Jew and Gentile; and thus Athanasius promotes our confidence in their early diffusion, their extraordinary importance and their Divine inspiration.

(4) *The Divisions in the Arian Party.*

In order to explain the origin and occasion of one of the noblest works of the illustrious exile, his *Epistle concerning the Synods of Rimini and Seleucia,* it is necessary to review in part the violent and petulant controversies which led to the calling of those councils. The flight of Athanasius and the induction of the truculent George into his vacated see at Alexandria apparently extinguished for the moment the candle of Nicene orthodoxy. In reality it brought to activity the violent antagonisms which were fermenting in the great coalition of Arian, semi-Arian and conservative parties of the East, and the oppressed and mystified churches and ecclesiastics of the West. The Western Churches had not in reality gone over to the enemy; but the extreme violence of Lucifer of Cagliari, and the approximation to something very like the Sabellianism of Paul of Samosata in the opinions of Marcellus, gave new energy to the semi-Arian party, and also at the same time forced into fresh prominence the extreme position which the ultra-Arian advocates had been doggedly pursuing.

The dogmatic positions of Arius were known to have been repudiated and anathematized by the great Council of Nicæa in 325, and the semi-Arian or Eusebian party fought for thirty years, not so much to reverse or undo the grave decisions of Nicæa, as to blacken the character of Athanasius and others who were the resolute defenders of the Homoousion. They shrank from the negative and positive assertions of Arius as little better than blasphemies, although they had accepted the aid of his followers in harassing and excommunicating the friends of Athanasius. But these irreconcilable Arians looked with extreme disfavour upon the elastic formulæ of the semi-Arians. Aetius was their leader and their most prominent advocate; but his secretary and amanuensis, Eunomius, afterwards Bishop of Cyzicus, gave his name to the movement. The latter was the rationalist of the fourth century, and was a man of mental integrity, and cold, dry reasoning faculty, as well as of moral earnestness and consistency. He pressed the extreme position that the Father alone was absolutely God, that any attempt to transfer Godhead to the Son of God was unthinkable. Eternal generation was absolutely inconceivable to him. If the Son was produced from the essence of the Father, it must have been at a definite point in time. This begotten and temporal nature was essentially *unlike* the substance of the Father, and he maintained that the term *Homoiousion* was even more unsatisfactory than the *Homoousion*. The two (οὐσιαι) substances were to him *anomoioi*, dissimilar, and hence the term *Anomœans, Heterousians, Exeecontians*,[1] were given to them or accepted by them. The Father knows Himself as unbegotten, and the Son knows Himself as the begotten. The Son or Logos is the creation of the Divine energy or will, *by whom* henceforth the Father has created all things.

This of course drew a distinction between the Divine essence and His will; the one was absolute and eternal, the other relative, limited and temporal; the issue of which appeared to Homoousians to have been scarcely distinguishable from Manichæanism, and to be on the high road to pagan polytheism.

Eunomius smote violently the position of the semi-

[1] The two latter terms preserving the formulæ (ἐξ ἑτέρας οὐσίας), or creation from ἐξ οὐκ ὄντων.

Arians as well as that of the Athanasians, by declaring that the nature of the Godhead was *perfectly comprehensible*, and that there need be no mystery in the statements concerning it. All who maintained the contrary were said to be in utter ignorance of the first principles of Christianity. Christ, said he, was sent forth to draw men to the Father, and in obeying His summons we soar above and behind the generation of the Son, and obtain that knowledge of the only true God which is eternal life. Intellectual apprehension of God was with the Anomæans the sole subjective method of securing communion with God. The schoolman, the teacher, rises in his theory far above the priest, discourse takes precedence of sacrament, mental illumination is far in advance of ascetic devotion, and direct perception of God, is better than all liturgical worship.[1]

These views were equally hateful to Constantius, to the party of Athanasius, and to that of the triumphant semi-Arians. Constantius was ready to condemn Eunomius, and he was ultimately deposed by a council held at Constantinople in 360. He did not accept the deposition, but formed a schismatic sect of his own, which lasted until the next generation.

But in the year 357 the famous Ursacius and Valens held a synod at Sirmium, on the Danube, which formulated a statement of belief that was virtually the embodiment of the Anomæan contention, and which strongly repudiated the term $οὐσία$ or its compounds from the phraseology of divines. The outspoken and extreme Arianism of this Sirmium manifesto alarmed the entire West, and Phœbadius of Agen wrote a

---

[1] See Dorner's *Doctrine of Person of Christ*, Div. 1., ii. 264. Neander, iv 77. Clark's translations.

vigorous denunciation of these Anomæan tactics and rallied the reverence of the Gaulish churches. At the same time the conservatives of the East were fairly indignant at the audacity of the rationalists who had sheltered themselves under their shadow. Ursacius and Valens had access at this moment to the Emperor, then in the zenith of his popularity. The Eastern bishops were mortified at the fact that, though they had been fighting against Sabellianism and Homoousianism through the best part of a generation, it was only to find a treacherous pitfall at their feet. They called a synod of their own adherents, not numerous but weighty, at Ancyra, under the presidency of Basil, in 358, and defined their position in reference to the Son of God with extreme precision, and (except that they still anathematized the hated words) almost the whole of their statement, with the exception of the last anathema, was accepted by Hilary in an orthodox sense.

Moreover, even Athanasius was willing to accept their positions as virtually right; and, at all events, he postponed any effort to press the Homoousion upon them; and though not ready to waive the use of it, yet we have seen that in the four discourses he almost studiously adopts other and more circuitous methods of expression.

The deputation which the Eastern bishops sent to the court still being held at Sirmium once more won Constantius over to their side, and led to a third council at Sirmium, in which, while no new formula was fashioned, the recent Sirmian manifesto was suppressed, the fourth Antiochian symbol of 341 was accepted. It was this which Liberius was prevailed upon to sign, and upon the faith of which signature, after two years of suffering for the cause of Catholic doctrine, he was sent back to Rome.

So once more the semi-Arians gained a complete victory, but used it badly. Philostorgius (*H. E.*, iv. 8) tells us, with some exaggeration, that some seventy Arian bishops were sent into exile.[1] Among them were Eudoxius of Antioch, Aetius, Eunomius of Cyzicus and others. Many time-servers, like Ursacius and Valens, Macedonius of Constantinople, turned towards the semi-Arian leaders for support; and some of the exiles, on further hearing of their case, were restored to their sees.

The curious fact appears that at this moment the conservative leaders, like Basil of Ancyra and George of Laodicea, practically surrendered their prolonged remonstrance against the word οὐσία, and maintained that '*likeness in everything*' must include 'essence'; that if the word οὐσία were not to be found in Scripture, nevertheless the idea pervades it, and is virtually involved in the great name of God (ὁ ὤν, the existing One, 'He who is'). In using this argument they gave up objection to the use of the word *homoousion*.

Thus the several parties were strangely shifting their ground. The semi-Arians, the Homœans, the Anomœans, and the Homoousians were approaching and receding from one another as in some tangled dance, where court intrigue and personal ambition were blended with various and conflicting passions.

In 359 the Emperor, at Basil's request, called a council of the whole Church to decide finally on the doctrine which should be held by all alike. There was not one sharp question to be decided, as at Nicæa, but

[1] Mr. Gwatkin shows that though Nicenes began the persecuting process in connection with Arius and others, even if Athanasius himself was opposed to it (see above, p. 92), yet that nearly all the semi-Arian leaders sanctioned or practised it. —*Studies of Arianism*, p. 163.

a group of carefully balanced queries. The first intention was to hold the synod at Nicæa, but some feared that the very place might unduly influence their decisions. Then Nicomedia was decided upon, but before the bishops could gather there, the city, with its splendid cathedral and palace, was reduced to utter ruin by an earthquake, in which the Bishop Cecrops fell a victim. When then the bishops were on the point of assembling at Nicæa after all, counter orders were received that they were to divide themselves into two groups; the Western bishops were to gather at Ariminum, or Rimini, on the shore of the Adriatic, not far from Ravenna; and the Easterns, with those of Africa and Thrace, at Seleucia, the capital of Isauria, a few miles from the Cilician seaboard. The plan of the secret Anomæan party, of Ursacius and Valens, included the preparation of a draft and creed for the double synod which should be broadly acceptable to the court and the semi-Arians, and at the same time should not openly condemn the Anomæans; and these wily men persuaded the semi-Arians to join them in drawing up a formula for presentation to the assembly.

That semi-Arians who had been drawing towards the Nicene party should in this manner demean themselves was a lamentable lowering of the whole controversy. The document, after long debate, was drawn up at Sirmium, and is sometimes called the Fourth of Sirmium, but more currently 'the Dated Creed.' Athanasius, in his treatise *Concerning the Synods*, severely comments on the simple fact of its having a date and appending the names of the consuls as if date had anything to do with the faith of the Church of Christ.

The creed is preserved by Athanasius and Socrates (*H. E.*, ii. 37). It declares 'that the Father is unbegotten, the Son the only begotten of the Father, before

all ages, or beginning or conceivable time, God from
God *similar* (*Homoion,* not *Homoousion,* nor *Homoiousion*) to the Father,' etc. It then proceeds to denounce
the use of the *ousia, i.e.,* essence or substance, because
the word occasions scandal, and is not contained in
Scripture. It repeats, however, that the Son is *similar*
to the Father *in all things.* Valens tried to shirk the
clause ' in all things,' while Basil added a sentence
with a view of emphasizing the clause obnoxious to the
Anomæans.

With a letter from Constantius in their hands,
Ursacius and Valens, the time-serving advocates of
what was now called the Homœan party, reached
Rimini, and there found from two to three hundred
bishops awaiting them, for the most part resolute in
their determination to uphold the original Nicene
formula, and to pronounce the anathemas upon Arius,
and *a fortiori* on the Anomæans. They forwarded
this result of their deliberations back to the Emperor,
and asked to be sent back to their pastoral work.
The Homœan leaders, with the small Arian minority,
made their own separate report and deputation. The
letter of the council to the Emperor is a scathing
condemnation of Ursacius, Valens, Germinius and
others, who had so repeatedly shifted their ground,
apparently with no higher principle than self-interest.
According to Sulpicius Severus, the orthodox deputies
were young and inexperienced, while the Arians had
chosen astute men, who could more easily persuade
Constantius. One of the most puzzling facts is, that
—perhaps worried at Hadrianople by delay in being
permitted to see Constantius, who was then in sore
anxiety about the Persian war and the fall of Amida,—
the deputies of the Council of Rimini were cajoled
by these arch-diplomatists, Ursacius, etc , to sign a

THE VICTORY OF THE HOMÆANS.

modified form of the Homæan manifesto, with an added caveat against the use of the term *hypostasis* as well as *ousia*, and with the omission of the clause 'in all things.'

By some mysterious sophistry or various threats, Valens contrived further, on the return of the deputation to Rimini, to induce the council there to sign the Arian Creed. The humiliation of this council was complete.

While these things were going on at Rimini,—the full particulars of which, we conclude, had scarcely reached the hidden retirement of Athanasius, as he is comparatively silent about them,—the Eastern bishops assembled at Seleucia, near Tarsus, to the number of 150 or 160. These mostly consisted of the blended conservative and semi-Arian parties, with about forty of the Acacian and Anomæan bishops, and a few Nicenes from Egypt. Hilary of Poitiers was summoned to Seleucia by reason of his being at that time an exile in Phrygia, and there he was a host in himself. He contrived to draw the lines more closely between the semi-Arians and the Nicenes.

The proceedings were turbulent and confusing. The Anomæan party was headed by Acacius of Cæsarea, Eudoxius of Antioch, and George of Alexandria. The semi-Arians numbered George of Laodicea, Basil of Ancyra, and Cyril of Jerusalem, the latter of whom scarcely differed at all from Nicene orthodoxy except in the non-use of the word 'consubstantial' (*homoousion*), as a term involving Sabellianism. It might seem that the Anomæan party was entirely out-numbered by two to one; yet, with the courage of despair, Acacius boldly demanded the abolition of the Nicene symbol, and the production of a new formula, which should embody the Sirmian manifesto. The Acacians declared that 'the Christ was a creature in no way similar to the Divine Essence.'

The strength of these blasphemous expressions roused the courage of the semi-Arians. Sylvanus of Tarsus moved that no new manifesto was needed, but that one of the documents of the Synod of Antioch be reaffirmed: on this the strict Arians withdrew. The secession imperilled the continuance of the council, and we have conflicting statements concerning the proceedings of the second and third days. The upshot of them was that Acacius, again trimming his course, proposed a creed not unlike the third Sirmium formula, in which the Anomæans were anathematized and the Homæan catchword introduced; and by these means he separated the small party to which he professedly belonged, into two groups. Acacius was thus nominally on the side of the majority. After boundless discussion and changes of front, representatives of both synods were prevailed upon to sign a Homæan creed, even Acacius and his party consented, as well as the more unmanageable chiefs of the old conservative and Homoousian parties. This was the memorable occasion of which Jerome, writing (*adversus Luciferanos*), exclaimed, *Ingemuit totus orbis et Arianum se esse miratus est* (The whole world gave forth a groan, and was astonished to find itself Arian).

The reader may probably be amazed to find the rapidity with which the term 'Homæan' took possession of ecclesiastics who had been contending for a quarter of a century over the application of the word *homoousios*, or *homoiousios*, to the Divine Son, and still more that any who had dared to accept the position that the Essence of the Father was absolutely *unlike* that of the Son, should have been induced to accept the *homoios*, which seems like a categorical repudiation of the very term *anomoios*. Some light, however, is thrown upon the strange phenomenon, by remembering that the acceptance of the Homœan compromise was a stepping-stone to Arianism proper on the part of some, and a solace for troubled conscience on the part of others. It was elastic in the last degree. It might mean all that Athanasius contended for—the absolute and eternal Deity of the Son of God; it might be supposed to be identical with the semi-Arian homoiousios, but it might be so watered down in meaning as to resolve itself into assertion of the creature condition of the Son, and connote merely a likeness of spirit or will or purpose, and be compatible with pure Unitarianism.

The compromise seemed to offer peace to the Church, but none can read the vigorous pages of Athanasius' historical and theological letter or treatise *Concerning the Councils at Ariminum and Seleucia* without discovering the hollowness of the truce. Mr. Gwatkin (*Studies*, etc., p. 176) observes : ' Athanasius rises above himself in his *De Synodis*, he had been a champion of controversy since his youth, and spent his manhood in the forefront of the hottest battle. The care of many churches rested on him, the pertinacity of many enemies wore out his life. Twice he had been driven from his see, and twice come back in triumph ; and now, far on in life, he found his work again destroyed, himself a fugitive. We do not look for impartiality in Demosthenes or Mazzini, and cannot wonder if even Athanasius grows more and more bitter and unjust to the authors of his exile; yet no sooner is he cheered with the news of hope than the jealousies of forty years are hushed in a moment, as though the Lord had spoken peace to the grey old exile's troubled soul. To the impenitent Arians he is the same as ever, but for old enemies returning to a better mind he has nothing but brotherly consideration and respectful sympathy.'

Of his great treatise, the first chapter is an able and exhaustive *résumé* of the court intrigue, which dreaded a fresh anathema upon heresies condemned at Nicæa, and adopted tactics which, when looked at reflectively and historically, are thereby condemned. The collation of the numerous Arian manifestoes becomes the witness to the lack of earnestness and honour which characterized the marshalling of the treacherous allies. The thirteen or fourteen documents which he places one after the other with illustrative comments are a striking contrast to the Nicene doctrine, which he in later chapters describes with great precision and acumen.

Acacius had won a great victory. It seemed that the Homæan compromise was accepted on all sides, and had to be followed up by the deposition of the Anomæans like Aetius, and Eunomius, who had refused it, and by the humiliation of the semi-Arians, who had positively accepted it. Acacius reverted to the tactics with which Athanasius, Marcellus, and Eustathius, had been silenced in earlier years. He brought charges of moral offence or ecclesiastical laxity against Macedonius of Constantinople Basil of Ancyra, Cyril of Jerusalem, Eustathius of Sebaste, and many others. This was done at a synod held at Constantinople in 360. The Emperor confirmed these infamous sentences, and with violent threats the synod sent the Seleucia-Rimini Creed for signature to all the bishops in Christendom. They placed Eudoxius in the bishopric of Constantinople, and in 361 he was followed by one of the original friends of Arius, Euzious. It was from the hands of the latter that Constantius received baptism just before he commenced a march westwards to crush the pretensions of his own nephew, Julian.

(5) *The Divinity of the Holy Spirit.*

Athanasius did not limit himself to one doctrinal theme or one ecclesiastical dispute. Several letters of his, written towards the very close of his prolonged exile, are still extant. To one of these we have already referred—his Epistle to Serapion concerning the death of Arius, more appropriately introduced at an earlier portion of our sketch. After the deposition of Macedonius, who had made himself obnoxious to the triumphant Acacius, it appears that he and some others who held the Catholic doctrine concerning the Son of God, and separated themselves from the Anomæans, were advocating views touching the Holy Spirit even more perilous to the Divine Unity. The Spirit of God was declared not to differ from the angels of God in nature, but only in rank; that, in fact, He was simply one of the ministering spirits sent forth to minister to the heirs of salvation.

Athanasius was overwhelmed with anxieties of every kind and with the literary and epistolary efforts which have been recited, but he rose to the occasion, and he produced a most valuable treatise on the *Divinity of the Holy Spirit*, which, as well as an abridgment of it, is still extant. The genuineness of these documents was questioned by Erasmus and Rivet, but it is accepted by Tillemont.[1] The whole opening of the Subject shows how deeply rooted in the spirit of Athanasius, both as a sacred tradition and as a Scrip-

[1] *Memoires*, etc. . Notes, *Sur S. Athan*, 84.

tural revelation, was the idea of the Trinity in the Unity of the Godhead. He charges Macedonius with holding—on the hypothesis that had been explained to him—a Dyad rather than a Triad. He says, to class the Spirit among creatures dissolves the Trinity; and he charges the sin against the Holy Spirit upon those who dishonour His Divine and eternal majesty. He then proceeds to quote passages throughout Scripture which reveal the lofty and transcendent powers of the Spirit, and to grapple with the difficulty suggested by those which seem to imply a subordinate and created dignity. He draws a distinction between the references to the Spirit—which undoubtedly connote the Spirit of God, the Holy Ghost—and those which, without such adjuncts, refer to a created spirit of man or angel; and he quotes and comments on scores of passages where the Divine Spirit is portrayed with all the prerogatives of Deity. Even where the Father and Son are mentioned as the sublime Unity, the Spirit, he argues, is as much involved *in the Son,* as the Son is implied or implicitly suggested whenever the Father is mentioned alone. He develops also the view of the Holy Spirit as the active energy of the Logos in the prophets and before the incarnation; thus preparing the way for the views which the Western Church has held so tenaciously of the eternal forthcoming of the Holy Spirit from the Father and the Son. He does not find that the Spirit is ever regarded or spoken of as brother of the Son nor as the Father of the Son. The Spirit of the Father is identical with the Spirit of the Son.

CHAPTER XI.

THE ACCESSION OF JULIAN, AND THE THIRD RESTORATION OF ATHANASIUS TO HIS SEE.

THE character and career of 'the Apostate' Julian can only be referred to in this place so far as they tell upon the fortune and influence of Athanasius. A few pages are nevertheless indispensable to a right apprehension of the effect which this extraordinary episode in the history of the empire produced upon the Church at that moment of apparently triumphant Homœanism.

The literature of the period is abundant. The friends and enemies of Julian have vied with each other in photographing for us the man and his ways. With blind partiality or with bitter invective, with historical detail or with rhetorical inflation, they have told the story of his education and his sufferings, of his white heat of hatred to Constantius, his 'stormless bay of deep contempt' for Christianity and the Church. We hear of his military achievements, his passionate enthusiasm for the gods of Olympus, his revolting submission to the most loathsome ceremonial, his extravagant supernaturalism and his eclectic philosophy. One historiographer recounts his wit, his fanatical purpose and his occasional outbreak of good sense. Another, his grandiose reconstruction of polytheistic worship, order, and church, aping in some respects, and thus paying an unintentional flattery to, the community which he detested. Moreover he cherished a vain ambition to exceed the splendour of military achievement which made Alexander, Pompeius, Hadrian, and Aurelian great in popular regard; while to the more phlegmatic reader the manner of his fall recalls the romance of Alexander's death and the dignity of that of Socrates.

We are not left, however, to the labours of his contemporaries—to the history of Ammianus Marcellinus or the orations of Libanius, to the invectives of Gregory of Nazianzus or Chrysostom, to the early Church historians of every complexion, who pour out upon his memory the vials of their wrath. We have his own *Orations*, his *Letters*, his *Cæsars*, and *Misapogon*, which give us insight into his innermost life, displaying the rankling malice which sent a glow of luminous fire into the otherwise dark caverns of his chaotic experience.

Gregory of Nazianzus (*Orat. c. Pag.*, ii), quoted by Socrates (iii. c. 23), gives a contemporary's account of Julian's personal appearance and manner that is more than a photograph. He is speaking of Julian's residence in Athens before he was raised to the rank of Cæsar. 'I well remember that even then I was no bad diviner concerning this person, although I by no means pretend to be one of those skilled in the art of divination; but the fickleness of his disposition and the incredible extravagancy of his mind rendered me prophetic, if indeed he is prophetic whose conjectures are verified by subsequent events. For it seemed to me that no good was portended by a neck seldom steady, the frequent shrugging of the shoulders, an eye scowling and always in motion, together with a frenzied aspect, a gait irregular and tottering, a nose breathing only contempt and insult, with ridiculous contortions of countenance;

explosions of immoderate and very loud laughter, nods as it were of assent, and drawings back of the head as if in denial, without any visible cause, speech with hesitancy and interrupted by his breathing, disorderly and senseless questions, with answers of a corresponding character, all jumbled together without the least consistency of method; . . . and I exclaimed then, "Ah, how great a mischief to itself is the Roman empire fostering!" and I prayed at the same time that I might be a false prophet.'

Of no other Roman Augustus do we really know so much. This is the more remarkable, since his stupendous failure to destroy the Church and rehabilitate the Homeric gods and the Platonic philosophy ran its course in the extremely brief period of little more than two eventful years.

Goaded by a sense of intolerable wrong done to him and his family on the accession of Constantius, forced by a fatality in his circumstances to study the masterpieces of pagan philosophy and poetry, and to taste the mysteries of theurgy, and the intoxicating draughts of eloquence which found their sources amid the temples and ritual of Athens and Eleusis, he early and secretly renounced the pollutions and impieties, as he deemed them, of Christian dogma and worship, and longed for the time when he might throw off the mask, and openly declare his unabashed loyalty to the 'immortal gods.'

This opportunity was found during his Cæsarship in Gaul, where with varied fortune he endeavoured to crush out rebellion on the banks of the Rhine. Julian had no leaning at this period towards the doctrine associated with the name and punished by the deposition of the great Athanasius, but he bitterly despised the controversy between the rival factions, and the cause or side of Constantius may have been presumably in his opinion the less honest and comprehensible of the two, although the Arian formulæ and temper of mind were felt instinctively by him to be more tolerant of his polytheistic eclecticism than the unbending monotheism of the great exile. His presence and known repudiation of all Christian dogma must have shaken, by the consciousness of impending change, the vigour of the aggressive Arianism of the court of Constantius. At all events, the threats that accompanied the presentation of the Arianized creed to the bishops of Gaul roused among them courage to resist the Homæan formula, and in the year 361 induced them to meet in synod at Paris, where they drew up a synodal letter to the Eastern Churches, and one which pronounced most explicitly and decidedly for the Nicene doctrine. The supposed pacification of the Church was therefore not accomplished, and no reconciliation was effected between the East and West. The mystification of the Western Churches vanished, though more than seventy years elapsed before the Homæan Compromise ceased to vex the churches of the East.

This is not the place to describe the victories of Julian, and the acclamations of the soldiery, which greeted him with the title of Augustus, nor how Constantius resolved to meet his nephew in arms, but was cut down by a short illness when not far from the fortress of Seleucia, where the council had been held.

Dr. Newman, speaking of this 'critical moment,' declares 'that the cause of truth was only not in the lowest state of degradation because a party was in authority and in power which could reduce it lower still; the Latins committed to an anti-catholic creed, the pope a renegade, Hosius fallen and dead, Athanasius wandering in the deserts, Arians in the sees of Christendom, their doctrine growing in blasphemy, and their profession of it in boldness every day. The Emperor had come to the throne when almost a boy, and at this time he was only forty-four years old. In the ordinary course of things he might have reigned till, humanly speaking, orthodoxy was extinct.'[1]

Julian, though known to be passionately pagan and avowedly anti-Christian in his sympathies, was indubitably the only member of the family of the great Constantine who could inherit his crown, and, having won the purple on the battle-field, he found none to dispute his accession to the undivided honours of the imperial throne.

One of the early events of his reign throws a lurid light upon the state of manners—upon the vehement passions that were stirred. We have already seen (p. 93) that George, the usurping occupant of the episcopal see of Alexandria, had made himself violently obnoxious, not only to the advocates of the doctrines of the Nicene Council, but to the heathen, who still formed a powerful section of the population. Their gorgeous temples, libraries, museums and works of art were still the most noticeable features of the great city, and roused the scorn and provoked the truculent disposition of George. More than once he had made himself so supremely hateful to the people generally that he was glad to fly from the dangers of his own episcopal seat. He had been busy at the Council of Seleucia, and must have been won over to the Homœan formula; for if not, some efforts would have been taken by Acacius to suppress him. He returned to Alexandria, however, unmollified in his iconoclastic mood.

[1] *History of Arians*, 3rd edit., p. 362.

He was heard to point to one of the temples and to ask, 'How much longer is this sepulchre to endure?' Constantius had been wishful to destroy it, and George resolved to erect upon its site a Christian church.[1] The Christians were stirred to the violent measure of ransacking the shrine and revealing all the shame, the defilement, the dead men's bones, and instruments for deception used in pretended mysteries that had been enacted there. The pagans, partly in reprisal for this exposure, and probably counting upon the favour of the pagan emperor, made a furious onslaught on the Christian population; many were beaten to death, some were crucified and a great multitude were wounded. They even seized George the Archbishop, and under their atrocious ill-treatment he succumbed. It seems doubtful whether it was his wounded body or his corpse that they led in triumph on the back of a camel through the long and splendid street of the city. His body was consumed to ashes with that of the beast which carried him, and they were cast into the sea. To the honour of Julian be it said, that he resented this violent outbreak of pagan violence. One of his extant letters contains his reprimand.

It is preserved by Socrates (iii. c. 3). We find, however, that while bitterly remonstrating with his

---

[1] Tillemont (vol. viii. p 201) seems to think that this event corresponds so closely with the ransacking of the Adytum of the Serapeum, described by Rufinus as taking place in the reign of Theodosius, that the two events may have been confounded. Socrates and Sozomen both refer it to a disused place in the city, once consecrated to the worship of Mithras, on which Constantius and George alike wished to build a church, but in the substructures of which the Christians found a vast subterranean recess filled with abominable memorials of magic art and heathen worship.—*Socrates*, iii. c. 12.

subjects for the administration of lynch-law, he slyly observed, 'You will no doubt be ready to say that George justly merited this chastisement; and *we* might be disposed perhaps to *admit* that *he deserved still more acute tortures*. Should you further affirm that on your account he was worthy of these sufferings, even this might also be granted. But,' etc., etc. . . 'we restrict ourselves to the mild and gentle medicine of remonstrance and exhortation;' and he winds up with a compliment to the Greek blood of our citizens of Alexandria!

The event had many consequences.

(*a*) The Arians, with their usual inveracity, accused the orthodox party and the friends of Athanasius of instigating or abetting the deed; but an abundance of evidence is forthcoming to demonstrate that it was perpetrated by the heathen party alone. Doubtless the impression was made that a new day of polytheistic worship and honours was about to dawn, under the patronage of a prince known to inspect the entrails of the sacrifices, and pay the most fanatic devotion at the shrine of the national gods.

(*b*) Christians began to fear the reutterance of persecuting edicts. Certain steps were taken to make the old religion the only form recognised by the State. The palace was cleared of Christians. Bishops, eunuchs, cooks and barbers, with heads of monasteries, were packed off, 'bag and baggage.' Priests of Apollo and Poseidon, augurs, flamens, prophets, bards, philosophers were taking their place and receiving their emoluments. Much practical persecution took place, and the ancient temples in Greece and Asia Minor were once more prepared for worship. Property that had been confiscated had to be restored to the old cult. Christians were forbidden to study the Greek classics

or poetry, and were for the nonce deprived of the power
or right to educate their children. Alas, that similar
methods of galling persecution should have been
practised by dominant churches in Protestant Europe,
and far less than 1,500 years ago!

(*c*) The Arian churches and bishops felt it to be
incumbent upon them to appoint immediately a successor to George. It is said by Socrates (*H. E.*, iii. 4)
that he was at once 'consecrated'; but further evidence goes to show that this was not effected until the
death of Athanasius. At all events, they did select, as
their leader and spokesman, one Lucius, who was a
priest ordained by George. They needed to take some
steps, for *Athanasius was at the door*.

(*d*) The most striking immediate consequence or
sequence was an edict of Julian's, which, setting at
nought all the decisions of councils or synods of
ecclesiastics, gave permission to all exiled bishops to
return from their places of concealment and revisit
their flocks. He did not venture to reinstate them in
their offices. This may have been entirely beyond his
capacity, and he knew the limits of his power. He
did, however, order that their property should be
restored to them. The motive for this edict was
probably a contemptuous one. He sought to bring
the hostile elements in the Church and the personal
animosities that were unfortunately rife into direct
contact and collision, and thus to weaken the force of
Christian teaching by confusing its issues. Moreover
he had seen and heard enough of the consequences of
cruel persecution to make him dread the increase
of force given to Christian ideas by the glamour of
martyrdom; and he knew that reprisals and retaliation
were not impossible.

(*e*) Julian took another step, which corresponded

with the Declaration of Indulgence by which the Papist sovereign of the reformed kingdom of Great Britain endeavoured by dispensing power to liberate Roman Catholics from all impediments in the way of *their* worship, by granting religious liberty to Puritans, who for nearly a generation had been cruelly proscribed and punished. Julian's edict made the practice of every kind of religious rite and worship legal, and consequently allowed not only to the crushed Homoousian and the fanatic Anomæan, the Novatian and Donatist, the Gnostic and Manichee, abundant privileges, but also to the suppressed and impoverished heathen, who since the accession of Constantine to supreme power had been drinking the dregs and reaping the harvest of their own cruelties. Heathen worship, though attempted on a grand scale, was for the most part a miserable failure; and the apathy of the populations, their unwillingness to take any part in the pomp or to provide the necessary oblations, roused the bitter resentment of Julian. Though he did not condemn Christians to the wild beasts, nor holy virgins to open dishonour by any law, yet cruel persecutions, the detail of which fill the pages of the historians and spice the invective of Gregory, occurred throughout Asia Minor and in parts of Syria. One of the methods by which he filled his treasury was the infliction of heavy personal taxation on all Christians.

Julian set himself two impossible tasks—one was to restore an empire to Rome, which was now threatened on all sides with partition, dislocation, and decay. He entirely overrated his military or strategic powers, planned his Persian campaign with great lack of foresight, sought to embody in his tactics a resemblance to greater commanders which was entirely superficial, and madly pressed forward in a way which, if it had not led him to his doom, would have anticipated the disasters of succeeding reigns.

Moreover, he sought to extinguish Christianity by arguments which had failed in the hands of far more able and accomplished disputants. He was blind to the crowning excellencies of the religion and example of Christ, and could not see that the question now was not, 'What shall be done to Him that is called the Christ?' or 'Is there any Holy Spirit?' These questions would not have been unseasonable in the days of Celsus and Porphyry, but they had been irrevocably answered by the enlightened conscience. The Lord Christ *was* enthroned in the hearts of men. The mighty Holy Spirit was revolutionizing the world; and the burning question that alone thrilled the conscience of mankind at that epoch was, What is the limit of the worship of the Son of God? Is His glory so great as to unveil the essence of the Eternal Father, or was His rank in the universe only that of a derived and created deity? Down deep in the very hearts and inmost conscience of millions Christ was God and Lord of all; the controversy that raged was this, Is His Godhead absolute? and if so, have we one God, or three Gods?

A new power, because a new revelation, had gone forth, before which the impurities of heathenism could not stand. The very violence of theological controversy proved that polytheism was dead, and had been utterly supplanted. The new life, the saintly purity, the catholic charities and discriminate humanities which had arisen, confounded the selfishness of paganism. The incidental outbreak of the fierce and uncompromising foe, whose spirit Arian and Catholic were not so bold as to ignore, brought all that bore the Christian name into common lines, and revealed the vast extent of that Divine life which was initiated in the incarnation, and which, like leaven hidden in the meal, was slowly indeed but surely leavening the whole lump. Even the philosophy of Julian, such as it was, proved to be a helpless jumble of Nature-worship and Platonic philosophy, with an occasional but ghastly parody on Christian metaphysic. Favour was shown to the Jews, and permission given to rebuild the Temple on Zion. This project was strangely if not supernaturally arrested; and the event produced a profound impression that a Power mightier than the Roman legion, more subtle than oriental magic, more invincible than the Homeric gods, was contending with the apostate for the empire of the world.

CHAPTER XII.

THE ACTS OF ATHANASIUS ON HIS REAPPEARANCE AFTER HIS SIX YEARS OF EXILE.

ATHANASIUS took advantage of the edict of indulgence, and reappeared in Alexandria, to the great joy of his flock, February 22nd, 362.[1] Gregory describes his entrance as a conqueror riding upon an ass, amid inconceivable raptures not unlike those which accompanied his previous return from shorter periods of exile. The churches were at once placed at his dis-

[1] This date is that arrived at by several independent processes, notwithstanding the statement of Ammianus Marc.

posal, and the Arians were fain to solemnize their
worship in obscure and unknown places, under the
direction, though not the episcopal authority, of the
Lucius whom George had ordained to the priesthood.
Athanasius indulged in no act of retaliation, used no
weapons, not even the whip of rushes, to cleanse the
temple of the Lord. He was a prince of mediators,
and proceeded to reconcile those who were opposed to
each other, or who had some grievance against himself.
On a public occasion he read large portions of his
Apology for his Flight, in which he not only justified
his conduct, but repudiated utterly for himself or
others the principle of physical force. The sublime
teaching to which he had consecrated his life concerning
the Unity of the Eternal Trinity was like a lamp
placed on its pedestal, and the doctrine was once
more preached in the city without let or hindrance.
Gregory says, 'that as he had the force of the diamond
to resist the machinations of his foes, he had the
attractive energy of the lodestone to reunite those
whose relations with each other had been strained.
Some he applauded, others he gently reproved. He
roused the indolent, and repressed the exuberant
manifestations of the rash. He taught the ignorant
and feeble how to tread the difficult path of loyalty to
Christ, gave them precautions lest they should err;
and with gentle wisdom showed them how to retrace
steps that were perilous, and to rise again if they had
already fallen.' Thus wrote the eloquent Gregory of
Nazianzus concerning his friend.

that the martyrdom of Artemius preceded the murder of
George, and that this event followed Julian's arrival at
Antioch. See here special note in Mr. Gwatkin's *Studies of
Arianism*, cf. Dr. Bright, art. 'Athan.,' *Dict of Chr. Biog.*
Tillemont does not see his way to place it before *August*, 362

Athanasius emerged from his hiding-place in the Libyan desert; so also did the fiery Lucifer of Cagliari and Eusebius of Vercellæ, who had been in similar retreat in the recesses of the Thebaid. They met at Thebes itself, even then in many parts displaying the colossal ruins that we can trace to-day, and there arranged their course of action. Lucifer went to Antioch, to promote there the cause of the Nicene orthodoxy, and Eusebius turned to Alexandria to consult with Athanasius. They would probably float, sail, or row down the Nile together, rejoicing in their liberty. On arriving at the Delta their routes would diverge.

Shortly afterwards, at Alexandria, a synod of the greatest interest was held, at which were present twenty bishops who had been previously chased from their sees by George. They were all of them men of mark, of principle, and Christian patience, and they proceeded to discuss matters of commanding interest to the Church. This gathering, though inconspicuous in number, yet proved to be one of the most weighty councils that were ever held, not only for the sanctity and wisdom of its constituents, but for the quality and value of its decisions.

The first question discussed was the reception into the Church of those who had been entangled with Arian sympathies, or forced into heretical communion by wiles or by pressure they could not resist. Some, with almost Novatianist rigour, would have refused to the most penitent such recommunion as would have justified a resumption of any clerical office. But better counsels prevailed. The spirit of the parable of the Prodigal Son was cited by the majority, and they came to the resolution that if any had been forced by power which they could not have resisted to espouse Arian tenets, and were now prepared to repudiate them, they should retain their ecclesiastical dignities and offices. Leaders or defenders of the heresy who had taken active part in the conflict were, if repentant, received to Church privileges on condition of their anathematizing the Arian heresy and its supporters; but even these were not confirmed in their ecclesiastical offices. These resolutions were communicated to and affirmed by Liberius of Rome; and numerous synods in Gaul, Spain, and Greece passed similar ones.

The *second* question arose out of the contention of some who were prepared to accept the Nicene definitions, that they were at liberty to hold that the Holy Spirit was a *creature*. It was against this dislocation of the Trinity that Athanasius, during his exile, had written the letter to Serapion, of which an outline has been given. It will be remembered that the Nicene Creed on this profound subject was in its original form exceedingly concise. The article was, 'I believe in the Holy Spirit.' Athanasius contended that this bald statement carried the consubstantial Divinity of the Spirit, but he argued the point, as we have seen, by the abundant language of Scripture, and deduced it from the already conceded conception of a Trinity in Unity, which, whatever had been the explanations attempted by the Sabellians or Origenists, Arians or Homæans, had not been repudiated. The synod declared that the Holy Spirit was of the same substance and Divinity with the Father and the Son, and that in the Trinity there was nothing of the nature of a creature, nothing lower or later. They felt that the whole controversy concerning the person of the Lord Jesus Christ would reappear in the endeavour to define the nature of grace or inspiration, and in the Divine opera-

SYNOD OF ALEXANDRIA. 143

tions in the Church and in individuals. Anomæans and Arians were of course by parity of reasoning ready to assert the derived and creaturely quality or essence of the Spirit, the Sabellians to fall back on pantheistic confusion of the Father and the Spirit, and the conservatives and semi-Arians to draw some kind of distinction between the Deity of the Son and the Spirit. Athanasius felt that the distinction of the Father and Son in the unity of the undivided Godhead must either be asserted with reference to the Spirit or abandoned altogether.

Another and *third* very important question was discussed by the Synod of Alexandria, under the direction of the great archbishop; and it is fairly cited to prove the moderating influence of Athanasius, and that he did not fight for words, but for realities. His position was, that whenever it was perfectly clear that opponents in a controversy were using words in different senses, but that in their hearts they were trying to accept and express the same spiritual reality, he could dispense with the *word* altogether, or justify his friends in using it in different senses.

The special difficulty which bade fair to divide even the Nicene confessors into two camps received practical and concrete expression at Antioch. In this city Meletius on the one side, and the Eustathians on the other, were unable to agree on the use of the theological term *hypostasis*. Meletius, as we have seen, was, towards the close of the reign of Constantius, after the Synod of Ariminum-Seleucia, appointed by the Homæans as the bishop (patriarch) of the great church in Antioch, under the belief that he accepted their formulæ. He had no sooner entered on his office than his bold assertion of the Nicene doctrine had excited the enthusiasm of his flock, but also aroused

the fanatical opposition of the Arian leaders, who at
once secured the banishment of the bishop whom they
had just elected, and the consecration in his place of
Euzoius, the early friend of Arius. This Euzoius, out
of respect for Paulinus, the unconsecrated *locum tenens*
of the orthodox and exiled Eustathius, had allowed
him to continue his services in a small suburban
church. On the accession of Julian, Meletius had
been encouraged to return to Antioch and resume his
functions. So that Antioch had now three parties.
First of all, the Arianized party, curiously compounded
of various sections of the Arians under the episcopate
of Euzoius, and two men who really held identical
views, namely the legitimate Bishop Meletius and the
orthodox preacher Paulinus.

The obvious course of wisdom would have been that
the Eustathians and Meletians should have combined
and agreed to accept the episcopate of Meletius, and
this notwithstanding certain theological differences
between them. Though the Synod of Alexandria had
wisely counselled this course, their advice came too
late, for Lucifer, the hot-headed, uncompromising
partisan, had gone to Antioch at the time when Eusebius of Vercellæ resorted to Alexandria; and although
he was profoundly interested in the complicated condition of the Antiochene church, yet he fomented the
discord which he should have endeavoured to heal;
and he aggravated the differences that he might have
explained away, and had actually made matters worse
by consecrating Paulinus Bishop of the Eustathians;
and so the schism in the church of Antioch was continued for half a century.

The point on which they differed represented two
tendencies in the Church, which were partly due to
the fact that Christian ideas had to be expressed, not

only in the Greek language, but also in Latin and Syriac; and some of these words suffered subtle changes of meaning as they were transferred with good faith from one language to another.

The word *hypostasis* has a varied connotation; thus, it meant fundamentally, that which 'stands under' a thing to cause its support, and answers very closely to the Latin word *substantia*. The latter, however, could not be used, as hypostasis was used, of 'the sediment at the bottom of a liquid,' nor, at first at least, of 'a person' in the sense of an individual. The Scriptural usage of the Greek word (say in Heb. i. 3) appears to express the *substance*, the reality of the Divine Being, apart from any special aspect, quality, affirmation, personality, contained or involved in that being. The Appendix to the Nicene Creed identifies the terms *hypostasis* and *ousia*. This last term means simply 'essence' or 'being,' and is the word constantly used by Athanasius when controverting the doctrines of the Arians. Consequently the Alexandrines and Homoousians continually spoke of one *ousia* as between the Father and Son, and even of the *one hypostasis* of the Father, Son, and Holy Spirit.

Now, this word had not been *transliterated* into the Latin language, but *translated*. Unfortunately, it was rendered by the Latin word *persona*, and very likely in good faith, because 'the Person' of God *may* have simply meant to them that which was most essential to Him. But the word *persona*, in Latin, had an etymological origin from *per-sonare* = *to blow or speak through*, as a mask; and *persona* came to mean, not simply the mask, but the *character* assumed by a man, one man being able to sustain several *personas*. Afterwards it meant an *individual*, as well as a '*character*.' This peculiarity of the word chosen to translate hypostasis natu-

rally suggested two diverse but perilous conceptions—
(a) that there were *three persons* in the Godhead, not in
the sense of three *realities*, but of three *characters*,
aspects, or qualities of the Godhead; and this was a
position which the Sabellians had treated as expressing
their whole doctrine of the Godhead, viz., that the
Father, Son, and Spirit were names adopted to express
the successive manifestations of the Monad. This was
sufficiently alarming to those who strongly held the
real distinctions between Father and Son, between
both and the Spirit. Nor (b) did the difficulty end
here, for many replied, 'Person' means 'individual,'
and therefore, three 'hypostases' must mean that there
are in the Godhead three *individuals*, viz.: 'Father,'
'Son,' and 'Holy Spirit'—an error antithetic to Sabellianism, leading at once to Tritheism.

The Asiatic Greeks generally used the term, three
'hypostases,' meaning by the term three internal
realities, not three transitory characters, nor still less
three Gods; and they did not hesitate to use their
Greek term for that purpose in opposition to the
Sabellian theory of *one hypostasis*. The Western
Church, after the rise of the Arian controversy, found
the Eastern speaking of 'three hypostases.' Now the
only translations they had of the word were either
'substances,' or 'characters,' or 'individuals.' First,
they felt that hypostasis could not mean *substance*, or
they would be favouring at once thereby some Arian
subtlety, some homoiousion, heterousion, or the like;
nor could they, secondly, take the word in the sense of
'*character*,' or they would be entrapped by the Sabellian hypothesis, of which they had been accused by the
Arians; nor could they, thirdly, take it in the sense of
'*individual*,' for then three 'hypostases' would mean
three 'Gods.' Therefore they were disposed to resist

the phrase altogether, and speak of *one* hypostasis, the very essence of the Trinity.

The word 'person' is just as perplexing and conducive to confusion or error at the present moment as it was in the fourth century. Theology does not mean by it now, nor did it then, an individual nor a mere characteristic. It ought not to be claimed as either tending to an obliteration or denial of the essential distinction between the Father and Son, nor to the idea that these are two in such a sense that they cannot be one. As a matter of fact and usage, the common use of the phrase 'three hypostases,' or 'three persons,' was far more current among the Arians than the orthodox; though it was used by the conservative party, and by the Arianized Catholics and Homæans. Consequently it was only natural that Meletius should have emphasized it. The Eustathians had, with the Western Church and Athanasius, insisted on the *one* hypostasis; and for this the Arians accused them of Sabellianism. Even before the Nicene Council, Hosius had strongly taken the same position, and at the Council of Sardica the strongest assertion was made in the same sense.

It must be noticed that Athanasius, though he preferred this usage, was far more than alive to the difficulty involved in it, and studiously avoided using mere technical terms whenever he could find a substitute for them. This mental habitude of his will perhaps throw light on the comprehensive spirit of the celebrated Synod of Alexandria, where the mind and temper of the illustrious Athanasius prevailed. The whole question was submitted to the assembly, and the *Synodal Letter*, which was sent to Antioch and elsewhere, first of all fell back on the Nicene formula, and suggested that no alteration be made in it; and went on to say of the two parties to this dispute, that, on inquiry, those who advocated the use of the phrase 'three hypostases' utterly repudiated the idea of 'three Gods,' and all similar conclusions; and, on the other hand, those who contended for the 'one hypostasis' avowed that they meant one *ousia*, and held that there was but *one*, because 'the Son is from the substance of the Father.' It was found that both parties were equally opposed to Arianism on the one hand, as to Sabellianism on the other, and both consented to the phraseology of the Nicene Creed, which does not decide the point in either sense by dogmatic formula. Would that theological controversy could always be adjusted by some such exercise of Christian patience and mutual compromise!

The word 'person' is a singularly unfortunate term, as it very frequently leads, even now, to serious misunderstanding. Those who use it intelligently do not mean that there are three *individuals* in the one God, nor that Father, Son, and Holy Spirit are merely *names* for one and the same Being; but they express by the term that there are indeed three distinct thinkable affirmations of reality in that Unity, that there are three internal and inherent relations, which enable the human mind to grasp the very idea of the Eternal ONE. In lack of a better term, the word 'Persons' of the Trinity connotes something vastly more than mere aspect, or name, or chronological development, or subjective distinction on our part, and something unquestionably less and other than 'individuality.' The Greeks regarded this word, hypostasis, as capable of application either (*a*) to the whole Godhead, which was thus said to be ONE, or (*b*) to the three stupendous conceptions of Father, Son, and Spirit, and which were thus said to be THREE.

Socrates (III. 7) informs us that the notable Synod

of Alexandria, under the presiding genius of its archbishop, had further occasion to discuss the ideas of Apollinaris the younger, who had sent representatives to Alexandria to advocate views which, in after years, severely harassed the Church. These views did not touch upon the great doctrine of the Godhead, but on that of the incarnation. The Apollinarians were believed to assert, that when the Son of God united Himself to humanity, He simply assumed the *body* of man—the eternal Logos taking the place of the human soul and intelligence. The immediate inference from this position would have been, that the humanity of Jesus was incomplete, that He was *not man*, but a *tertium quid*, neither God nor man. Now, man without human soul, or spirit, or intelligence, could neither be our Mediator nor our Saviour. It seems, however, that the monks sent by Apollinaris, when examined by the synod, admitted the Scriptural evidence for the human *soul* (psyche) of Jesus, but kept in reserve the apparently tripartite division of human nature referred to by St. Paul (1 Thess.v.23), and upon which Apollinaris had founded his thesis. While admitting the 'soul' of Jesus—the humanity to that extent of the Christ—he had denied the *spirit* or *intelligence* (*pneuma* or *nous*) of Jesus to be human, and urged that the place of such *spirit* had been taken by the *Logos*, the Eternal Word.

This aspect of the question was not pressed upon the synod, which felt that all that was essential had been conceded in the assertion of the human *soul* of the Lord Jesus. In this they lacked their general penetration and foresight, as the history of the next period of Church History abundantly proves.

The council resolved to send the synodal letter of peace and mutual remonstrance to Antioch. As we have already seen, their well-meant endeavours to harmonize the opposing congregations failed. Lucifer's conduct had rendered the union of the two communities impossible; and he was so enraged that he broke with both Eusebius of Vercellæ and with Athanasius, and took his departure to Sardinia. A sect of Luciferians was even prolonged into the following century. This must have been a source of bitter grief to Athanasius. The supposed 'Letters' of Athanasius to Lucifer have a very doubtful authenticity.

Now, as the affairs of the Eastern Churches were thus brought before Athanasius, he could not have been indifferent to the isolated cases of cruel persecution which were perpetrated partly to satisfy long pent-up rage in the breast of the heathen, and partly because it was believed to be well-pleasing to the pagan Emperor. Socrates says that he should require the pen of Æschylus or Sophocles to tell the hideous story of the sufferings of Marcus of Arethusa, brought upon him by a refusal on his part to rebuild a heathen temple at the instance of Julian; and every kind of indignity befell both Arians and Catholics, who put an obstacle in the way of the spasmodic reaction of paganism. The position of Athanasius must have been supposed tolerably secure, or we should not have heard the story (Ruf., ii. 28) that the relics of John the Baptist were sent to the Bishop of Alexandria for safe preservation. This transfer was made when the Pagans destroyed the church at Sebaste, which had in previous years been built to enshrine them.

A VIEW ON THE NILE.

CHAPTER XIII.

THE CAUSE AND ISSUE OF THE FOURTH EXILE OF ATHANASIUS.

THE ministry of the bishop was by God's grace exerting its magnetic power; and among other indications of its intensity, it is reported that three (heathen) Greek ladies had been converted and baptized by him, and that the news of the event was communicated to Julian. On this the Emperor burst forth in malediction. In restoring Athanasius he affected to suppose that he had not replaced him upon the episcopal throne. He scoffed and chafed at the obvious fact that Athanasius was virtual sovereign of Egypt. His recall was meant to have kindled fires of mutual hate among Christians. Unfortunately for Julian, however, the activity of this great man was the most powerful pacification of the opposing parties, or it became so dominant an influence that the Arian faction subsided into comparative obscurity and quiescence. The heathen party, which had been cynically rebuked for the *émeute* in which George was murderously lynched, were roused into passionate invective, and they assured Julian (Theod., *H. E.*, iii. 9) that, if Athanasius were allowed to remain in Alexandria, there would not be one pagan left, for that he led them all to espouse his own sentiments.

Gregory, in his orations, describes the effect thus: 'The devil found that it would be nothing to his advantage to conquer all the Christians, if Athanasius could not be overcome.' The success of his ministry forced from the eccentric and petulant Emperor the avowal that 'he hated (*Jul. Ep.* 6) Athanasius.' Socrates (*H. E.*, iii. 13) declares that the pagans of Alexandria (as well as of Athens) now proceeded to institute abominable mysteries, sacrificing boys and girls, inspecting their entrails, and even tasting their flesh. The dismay excited by the public and avowed celebration of these theurgic rites poured oil on the flame. Julian allowed all the other exiled bishops to remain at their sees, but took special means to crush and annihilate the influence of Athanasius. Doubtless he felt that there was much closer inner affinity between Arianism and his own faith, than between the Athanasian insistence on the Divine unity and solity and any form whatsoever of polytheistic doctrine or philosophy.

In a still extant letter, Julian (*Ep.* 16) sent a peremptory order for the immediate removal of this 'great foe of the gods,' on the ground that he had resumed his episcopal functions, to 'the utmost displeasure of all pious persons in Alexandria.' These 'pious persons' were the worshippers of the ancient gods of Egypt, Greece, and Rome; and all these knew that they could not be masters in a city which gloried in having Athanasius for its bishop. The general community of Alexandria, however, wrote a letter and also sent a deputation to Julian, eagerly remonstrating with him on the proposed deportation of their bishop.

The response of Julian to this appeal, which still remains, throws an interesting light on the exciting scenes that followed. Julian mocked the Alexandrians for their love to the Galilean and to His servant Athanasius, thus recognising that in a very special sense the cause of Christ and that of Athanasius were in his judgment identical. Julian's judgment is not

THE FOURTH EXILE.

worth much to anybody; yet, like the testimonies of Herod and Pontius Pilate and Judas to the innocence of the Lord Jesus from their standpoints, this cynicism of the Apostate is an unintentional testimony to the character and doctrine of Athanasius. The further admission came out, that the bishop was a primate of consummate ability, and had great powers of ruling men and managing affairs. Julian curiously admitted the power of Athanasius to interpret the Scriptures, and his readiness to risk his life for his faith, but bade them choose at once his successor to the episcopate. He also charged Ecdicius, the prefect, with blame for not having informed him already of the execution of the first order for the expulsion of Athanasius from Alexandria, and now with more vehemence than before commanded his banishment, not only from the metropolis, but from Egypt proper. He swore by Serapis, that if the bishop had not made himself scarce by December 1, he should demand a fine of a hundred pounds of gold from the officers of the prefecture. Moreover, ultimate and murderous designs were clearly and definitely suggested.

These communications were made to Athanasius on October 23, by Pythiodorus, a philosopher, and the bishop, not waiting for the month of grace, resolved on immediate departure. It was not a moment too soon, for a comparison of the histories of Socrates, Theodoret, and others makes it probable that Julian sent further officers with power to arrest and slay Athanasius. They did afterwards destroy with fire the greatest church (the Cæsareum) in the city, with the probable intention of destroying the bishop, whose place of concealment may have been, as they thought, some inner chamber in the church. On the arrival of these messengers, the followers of Athanasius gathered about him, terrified and distressed. He said with calmness: 'Let us retire for a while.' 'This commotion will quickly terminate; it is a cloud which appears and then vanishes away.' (Soc., *H. E.*, iii. 14; Theod., *H. E.*, iii. 9).

The Nile traveller, even of the present day, can easily recall the scene. The bishop, with a few attendants, slipped into a dahabieh on the shore of the lake or on the western branch of the Nile, and catching some favouring breeze, must have soon reached its junction with the main stream, and made headway towards the Thebaid. Theodoret says, he 'sailed to Thebes.' As his pursuers were in hot haste, it is hardly probable from the sequel that he had reached Thebes, a distance of some three or four weeks' sail. His attendants, who were aware of the pursuit, besought Athanasius to escape into the wilderness, which was dotted with the monastic seclusions that he knew so well. This retreat might have been possible at almost every turn of the river. However, his life was one long series of adventures. He had for six years baffled his pursuers, and was adroit in the art. 'Turn round,' said Athanasius, 'and let us meet our enemies.' The boat in which the fugitives were escaping up the river was turned about, and commenced the merry and rapid descent, with altered trim of sails, and other differences of appearance, which the modern traveller can so easily appreciate. Shortly afterwards, labouring up the stream, trecking by its banks, the bloodhounds were on their scent, and hailed the boat of Athanasius, as it, on the other hand, was probably with some impetuosity descending the mid-stream. 'Where is Athanasius?' they cry. '*He is near*,' was the reply, and they passed on. On the pursuers went; and the boat of Athanasius soon

reached the first station from Alexandria, called
Chœren; and there the Patriarch remained, so far as
public appearance went, in profound secrecy until
Easter of 363; and there too he composed his Festal
Epistle for that year.

During these few months Julian's failure to excite the
Antiochenes into any enthusiasm for ancient worship
had awakened his supreme disgust. At Antioch he
wrote the *Cæsars* and the *Misapogon,* and moreover
planned the Persian campaign so badly that he and his
reactionary mission vanished as a dream. Tillemont
supposes that he must have heard the rumour that the
object of his deadly hate was concealed in the neighbourhood of the city; and the last thing done before
starting on his journey for the Persian frontier was
to send special orders once more for the arrest and
death of Athanasius. The great confessor, on hearing
this, again entrusted himself to the river Nile, and
advanced towards the Thebaid.

It is possible that Athanasius reached the site of
'the hundred-gated city of Thebes,' walked amid the
ruins of the great temples at Karnak, and looked on
the columns which Ptolemy Lathyrus threw down in
his mad rage, and which still lie as he laid them, after
another 1,500 years. Probably he penetrated the
mysterious labyrinth behind the painted propylæa,
moved hushed and awed in the moonlight along the
avenues of the huge Hall of Columns, and gazed on that
petrifaction of the history and mythology of Egypt.
The statues of Amunoph were casting then their
shadows on the open spaces of the city; and the Mem-
nonium, though 1,800 years had passed over it, was in
its glorious beauty. In the savage gorge of the sepul-
chres of the Pharaohs, he may have hidden himself
from search amid some of the tombs which had even

then been despoiled of a whole series of tenants, and were used for the purposes of seclusion and monastic devotion. In one of these the present writer saw, still legible, in 1856 the remains of a portion of an encyclical letter of Athanasius, as well as signs of the Christian worship which had been practised during the Roman period in a building adjoining the great temple of Luxor. Whether or not our concealed patriarch did share in the mysteries of Christian song and communion in the No-Ammon of ancient Scriptures, we know that he visited the borders of the Thebaid.

One incident remains. On the northernmost limit of Upper Egypt was the city of Hermopolis Magna, and on the opposite and eastern side of the river, very near to the far-famed caves of Beni Hassan, was the city of Antinoe, erected by Hadrian in honour of his famous Antinous. Surrounding this city were numerous cells. Some of the very caves now visited for their unique archæological interest were occasionally used for the purposes of the recluses who had set up there the oriental type of the religious life. Pammon was their superior, and into one of these hiding-places Athanasius seems to have retired. During his residence Theodore of Tabenne, another illustrious abbot, came to visit him, and in the dead of night the three crossed the Nile to Hermopolis. They found the banks of the river crowded with bishops, presbyters and monks, with torches in their hands to welcome them. 'Who are these,' said he, 'who fly as a cloud and as doves to their dovecots?' Athanasius disembarked, and proceeded on an ass led by Theodore to the city. Here he remained for some weeks preaching and counselling the monks.

The pursuit must have been hot, for the two abbots

THE FOURTH EXILE.

urged Athanasius to hide again in the depth of Theodore's boat and hurry to the secrecy of his monastery at Tabenne. Wind and current were against them, and the only chance of advance was 'trecking' the vessel up the stream, a labour of love which the monks were eager to render. It is a touch of nature and authenticity which one story gives that during this process the hero of so many hairbreadth escapes should have been overcome by fear, and have given way to lamentation. Pammon encouraged his revered friend with the blessedness of being accounted worthy to suffer and to die for the name of the Lord Jesus. He was calmed by the faith of his companion, and God heard his own fervent prayers for grace. He then began to enlarge on the prospect of speedy execution. The two solitaries smiled at one another. Athanasius thought they were smiling at his tardy courage, when they communicated to him, as it would seem by sudden and inexplicable monition, the astounding intelligence that Julian had been slain in his Persian campaign.

The story goes that similar visions cheered the oppressed spirits of others at that time of sore anxiety. Thus (Sozom., *H. E.*, vi. 2)—Blind Didymus, an Alexandrine philosopher, had fasted and prayed, mourning continually over the pagan persecution of the Church; but now, being in an ecstasy, he beheld white horses traversing the air, and heard a voice saying, 'Go and tell Didymus that Julian has just been slain, and let him arise and eat; and communicate this intelligence to the Bishop Athanasius.' There are many well-accredited facts of a like kind which give an air of probability to these half-legendary accounts.

However, the news soon reached Alexandria, not only that Julian's star had set, and that the expedition had disastrously failed, but that Jovian, one of the most distinguished generals of the army, who had not renounced his Christianity, and who even favoured the Nicene doctrine, had been summoned by the army to take up the fallen purple. Thus 'the cloud vanished' and our hero once more appeared in Alexandria, and his fourth exile was thus brought to a termination. Letters from the new emperor, Jovian, in the summer of 363 A.D., bade him fully resume the dignities and responsibilities of his see. The letters, says Gregory (*Orat.* 21), were replete with admiration for the courage he had displayed in the maintainance of the faith and for the purity and sanctity of his life. But he did more, for he wrote a special letter entreating Athanasius to send him in writing exact instruction on the doctrine of the faith, as he was embarrassed by the multiplicity of sects and diversity of judgments.

We need not be surprised at Jovian's trouble. The soldier wanted orders, and the man personal consolation, as well as theological guidance. It seems doubtful whether the remarkable answer to this appeal was drawn up at Alexandria, with the assistance of a synod called for the purpose, or whether it was prepared in Antioch,[1] whither Athanasius unquestionably proceeded on September 5th of the same year. He was received by Jovian with great respect and courtesy. The dispute between Meletius and Paulinus had not been healed. Meletius was jealous and offended by the recognition of Paulinus, and friendly relations were not restored by the anxious mediation of Athanasius, who, as we have seen, believed and taught that the

---

[1] Baronius (*Ann.*, 363) and Valesius also think the former statement to be correct, on the authority of Theod., iv. 2.

doctrinal difficulty between them was merely one of words, not of things; that he could himself use the term one hypostasis of the Godhead in its fulness and unity, and also use the word as descriptive of the three several and distinct realities which constituted the ground of the relations between the Father, the Son and the Holy Spirit.

The document that was placed in the hands of Jovian became an ecclesiastical state-paper, a theological symbol and a literary treasure. It is preserved intact by Theodoret the historian, it contains and cites the text of the Nicene Creed, and it thus becomes one of the most indubitable authorities for the earliest form of that symbol; it also enables us to criticise some other documents which profess to expound it, and other summaries of Christian doctrine which have been attributed to Athanasius himself.[1] It further shows that Athanasius still thought the original form of the document was the best guide to the new Emperor in unravelling the mysterious conflict among Christians. It goes back and behind all the changes that had been suggested at Sardica or Antioch, Sirmium or Seleucia. It contained the central verity, to which, notwithstanding the fears of the orthodox after the Council of Ariminum-Seleucia, the immense majority of the churches adhered. Athanasius enumerated in his letter the Churches of Britain and Spain, Gaul and Italy, Macedonia and Greece, Pontus, Cappadocia, Egypt, Libya, and others; and declares that by correspondence with churches in all these lands he had learned their sentiments, and that with the exception of a few who advocated Arian doctrine this was

---

[1] See the text compared with that of the Creed of Eusebius of Cæsarea, p. 33.

the Catholic faith. The fact was that the Nicene definitions had never been repealed, and still held their ground. Liberius and hosts of bishops had eagerly renounced the Homæan formula when the heavy pressure of the hand of Constantius had been lifted.

During the short reign of Jovian the semi-Arians made known their views to the Emperor, and asked for a general council once more, in order to decide the often-debated question. The emergency was met by a synod held at Antioch in 364, when the leading Homæans, even Acacius, sat side by side with Meletius and Eusebius of Samosata, and forwarded a further letter to the Emperor which coincided almost verbally with the tenour of Athanasius' celebrated letter to Julian (Sozom., *H. E.*, vi. 4).

The Arian faction at Antioch, with the assistance of Lucius of Alexandria, made, notwithstanding, a vehement effort to prejudice the mind of Jovian against Athanasius, apparently taking up the old charges against him. Jovian would have none of it, and confirmed Athanasius in the full exercise of his episcopal functions.

The prospects now seemed brighter than they had appeared since the early triumph of the Nicene definitions or during any part of the complicated conflict which we have tried to explain.

Athanasius remained at Antioch till the spring of 364, when, after writing his Festal letter, he once more returned to Alexandria. The distress was doubtless very deep when the news reached the weary veteran that Jovian, after a short illness, had died in Bithynia, on his way to the capital. A dark and portentous shadow fell over the reviving prosperity of the Church. The coincidence was curious that at Nicæa the army should have summoned to the purple Valen-

THE FOURTH EXILE.

tinian, a general who had incurred the wrath of Julian by his outspoken repudiation of the heathen ceremonies which had been forced upon him. Valentinian was, like Jovian, a friend of the Nicene faith; but unfortunately he appointed, to the dignity and functions of the Augustus of the Eastern provinces, his brother Valens, who shortly afterwards became a bigoted Arian and open disciple of Euzoius.

Thus peace, which seemed to have been established, was at once broken. Attempts were once more made to force Anomæan and semi-Arian bishops on the churches of the East. Meletius was driven again from Antioch, and the vehement Euzoius lifted once more into his place. The Arians returned to their persecuting practices whenever they had a chance. It is even affirmed (Soc, *H. E*, iv. 2) that Valens caused many who refused communion with Euzoius to be drowned in the Orontes. Paulinus appears to have been left in peace (Soz, *H. E*, vi. 7), but many other of the orthodox bishops were cruelly treated. Yet for a while the storm did not break over Alexandria. Some who hold to the Athanasian origin of the *Life of St. Anthony* believe that it might have been written in the year 364 or 365. It is at least possible that Athanasius sent to Trèves the copy of the work that was for ages believed to have been written by him. This not long afterwards was read by the friends of Augustine, and it produced within that wonderful man a longing after the life of utter self-obliteration which has been called his conversion. Athanasius was thus one of the links which united East and West in the toils of the ascetic regimen.

CHAPTER XIV.

THE FIFTH EXILE AND CLOSING YEARS OF ATHANASIUS.

According to some authorities it was in the year 365, and to other documents 367, that the open policy of the Emperor Valens began to correspond with that of Constantius, and the edict was issued which reversed the policy of Julian, and ordered once more into banishment all who had been thus condemned by Constantius, even although they had been released by Julian. The order did not reach Alexandria that Athanasius should be displaced until May 5th of the year. The excitement produced was so great that the prefect sought to quiet it, so late as June 8th, by the promise to enquire especially from Valens as to the application of the general order to the case of the illustrious Athanasius. It was argued that the terms of the order did not exactly apply to him, as he had been banished by Julian and recalled by Jovian.

However, Valens was in earnest, and would not admit the validity of the verbal quibble. It seems as though a glamour of romantic achievement was to surround the Bishop of Alexandria to the end. The governor saw that the wishes of the Emperor could only be accomplished by force, 'for the people assembled in crowds, while commotion and perturbation prevailed throughout the city,' and, instead of carrying out the order for his removal, he gave time for the excitement to die down. On the night of October 6th, when the people were lulled into security and for the

PORTICO OF AN EGYPTIAN TOMB.

most part asleep, the military chiefs surrounded the church in which Athanasius generally dwelt, took possession of it, and proceeded with their search-warrant from basement to roof. Once more, nevertheless, the search was in vain. The skill and tact of the bishop, or the boundless affection and various contrivances of his personal friends—devices with which they must have been familiar through many years of cruel persecution—prevailed over the police, the magistracy, and the soldiery of the empire.

This last escape had a touch of supernatural mystery about it which wrought on the popular mind. For the moment it seemed like a divine rapture, and Sozomen says (*H. E*, vi. 12), 'More than human prudence seems to have been requisite to foresee and avoid such imminent danger.' Socrates (*H. E*, iv. 13) gives a more commonplace account of the transaction, and says that Athanasius, 'dreading the irrational impetuosity of the multitude, and fearing lest he should be regarded as the author of any excesses that might be committed, concealed himself for four months in his father's tomb.'

This little touch is one of the few hints we can gather of the family of this great man. His father's tomb was in the vicinity of the city. This implies residence in the neighbourhood, and sufficient means to secure a sepulchre of a size adequate for habitation.

The curious fact is that the Emperor, finding that the continued silence and absence of Athanasius kept the city in confusion and on the verge of seditious outbreak, and (as Sozomen adds) fearing now to excite the displeasure of his brother Valentinian, gave public permission for his recall.

One other touch brings out the extraordinary personality and magnetic force which appeared to emanate from the man. Sozomen says that for some reason not clearly explained 'the Arian bishops did not on this occasion plead vehemently against Athanasius.' His own theory was that they were afraid, if the prelate were not speedily reinstalled, that in some mysterious fashion they should find him to their dismay in the presence of the Emperor. Once there, he might work upon the mind of Valens and convert him to Nicene views, and be the means of utilizing the forces of the Western empire against themselves.

Whatever was the explanation, an imperial notary arrived with the order to reinstate Athanasius on his episcopal seat; and this was carried into effect for the fifth and last time, amid popular rejoicing, on February 1st, 366. Athanasius must have been then in his 69th or 70th year, and doubtless bore on his face the signs of his lifelong martyrdom. His mind was still as agile and his physical endurance as great as ever; while his literary projects, his philosophical discrimination, and his wide jurisdiction, were as remarkable as ever. Neither Arian machinations nor temporal power again molested his personal comfort or disputed the validity of his episcopate, and five more years were granted to him to pursue the grand purpose of his life. This was all the more remarkable because at Constantinople, Antioch, Samosata, and throughout the East the Arians kept up an irritating onslaught and bitter warfare on the defenders of the orthodox faith, and Valens was for the most part the instrument of their envy, malice, and uncharitableness. Cave[1] accepted the validity of the almost incredible story recorded by Socrates (*H. E.*, iv. 16): how that eighty clerics came to Valens to complain of ill-usuage from the Arians, and

---

[1] Lives of Primitive Fathers · *Life of Athanasius*, vol. ii. p. 189

how, while dissembling his real sentiments, he by a secret order gave authority to Modestus to arrest them and put them to death; how that the prefect, under the pretext of sending them by sea to various places of banishment, caused them to embark in a vessel which when in mid-sea was set on fire and totally consumed, the crew escaping by a barque which they had towed after them for this vile and treacherous purpose. Even if this be true, yet it is admitted on all hands that in Alexandria and throughout Egypt the faith of the Church and the followers and friends of Athanasius were left in peace. An attempt made by Lucius to establish a rival position in the diocese was frustrated, the populace rising, with the resolve to remove him from Egypt.

The labours of Athanasius were by no means at an end, and his Festal letter of 367 has a special value attributed to it, as it contains what has been called the *Canon of Athanasius,* or the list of sacred books of the Old and New Testaments. The document, or fragments of it, was extant in original Greek long before the discovery of the Syriac translation of the *Festal Letters;* and Mr. Cureton found in the British Museum another translation into Syriac of a large portion of the letter. The list of *New* Testament books shows that they were identical with those which we possess, and except that the General Epistles precede the Pauline, are in the same order as that with which we are familiar. Following the Hebrew enumeration of the Old Testament books, and thus reducing them to twenty-two, after the number of the letters of the Hebrew alphabet, he yet gives to the books their Greek titles as follows: (1) Genesis, (2) Exodus, (3) Leviticus, (4) Numbers, (5) Deuteronomy, (6) Joshua, (7) Judges, (8) Ruth, (9 and 10) four Books of Kings (meaning by the 1st and 2nd books those of Samuel, and by 3rd and 4th books our 1st and 2nd Books of Kings, as in the LXX., and reckoning the first two as one book, the last two also as one book), (11) the First and Second Books of Chronicles as one book, (12) two Books of Esdras as one = most probably to Ezra and Nehemiah, (13) Psalms, (14) Proverbs, (15) Ecclesiastes, (16) Song of Songs, (17) Job, (18) the twelve minor prophets as one book, (19) Isaiah, (20) Jeremiah, Baruch, the Lamentations and Epistle of Jeremiah as one book, (21) Ezekiel, and (22) Daniel.

These, says he, are 'the fountains of salvation, that he who thirsteth may be satisfied with the words they contain. In these alone is proclaimed the doctrine of godliness.' He then argues that the 'Wisdom of Solomon,' 'Wisdom of Sirach' (in the Syriac, 'of the Son of Sirach'), and 'Esther' and 'Judith' and 'Tobit,' the *Doctrine of the Apostles*, and 'the Shepherd,' may be read by those who come wishing for admonition and instruction in godliness. No mention is made of the Books of Maccabees, nor of the Epistle of Barnabas, nor of the Song of the Three Children, nor of the additions to Esdras, Esther or Daniel.

The chief difference as to the Canon of the Old Testament is in the high place assigned to Baruch and to the additions to Jeremiah; also the transfer of Esther to the second list, excluding it from the canon. It may be of special interest to observe that *The Doctrine of the Apostles* is cited,—a work the MS. of which has only come to light in the present generation, after being hidden from view for fifteen hundred years. As to the relative antiquity of Barnabas and the teaching or *Doctrine of the Apostles*, see Schaff's *The Oldest Church Manual*. This list shows very close approximation to the list found in Josephus, to those which are attributed to Melito by Eusebius, to those of Origen, Cyril of Jerusalem and others. The minute deviations with reference to the place of Lamentations, Baruch, etc., are carefully tabulated by Canon Westcott.[1] It is sufficient here to observe the link thus preserved of a grand traditional heritage of Holy Writ, and the opinion of the great theologian as to the 'fountains of truth and salvation.'

The closing words of the letter reserve for a third class the books which, without enumerating, he calls apocryphal, and on which the heretics were disposed to rely.

It is at least possible that at this period Athanasius wrote what was called *Expositio Fidei* (*ekthesis pisteos*) which the Benedictine editors of his works and Dr. Routh considered genuine, but which from much internal evidence has been seriously disputed. The ground of the hesitation has, with some editors, been mainly limited to the incompatibility of the doctrine with that of the so-called Athanasian Creed, particularly in respect of the repudiation of three *hypostases* of Father, Son and Holy Spirit, which that far-famed symbol distinctly formulates. In the light of the discussions that arose at the Synod of Alexandria, (see pp. 145, ff.), it would seem highly improbable that Athanasius should have formally pronounced against the idea of applying the word *hypostasis* to the realities of the Father, Son and Holy Spirit.

But there are many reasons for concluding that the commonly called *Creed of Athanasius*, the hymn or homily commencing *Quicunque vult*, did not receive its final form until the ninth century, and that the peculiar rhythm and series of antithetical sentences pervading

[1] Art 'Canon,' Smith's *Dictionary of Bible*, vol. i. p. 256.

long portions of the symbol are far more due to
Augustine than to Athanasius. Definite reasons exist
to show that the minatory clauses were added by slow
degrees, and that the doctrine and illustration of the
person of the Christ could not have been framed until
after the Nestorian, Eutychian, and Monophysite controversies of the fifth and sixth centuries.[1]

If 'the Creed of Athanasius' cannot be cited from
the theology of its supposed author, then the form of
the 'exposition of the faith' to which we refer cannot be repudiated on the ground of its dissimilarity;
and the genuineness of the *Expositio* would be another
reason for freeing Athanasius from all complicity with
the later document. I cannot but hesitate on many
other grounds to accept the authenticity of the *Expositio*, and the same thing may be said concerning a
work attributed to him at this period, and denominated
De Incarnatione et contra Arianos, from the difference
of its phraseology and style and even its theology from
another but undoubted document which was written
about the same time, viz., *Epistle to the Africans*.

The work on the Incarnation uses and justifies the
phrase '*three* hypostases,' in direct contradiction of
the repudiation of 'three,' and assertion of 'one,' in
the *Exposition*, whereas in the letter to the Africans
he speaks of one hypostasis; and in exegetical treatment of John iv. 28, he regards our Lord's language,
'the Father is greater than I,' as referring to the
human consciousness, and not to the eternal nature of
the Son of God. This letter was written to the
bishops in communion with him after the summons of
a synod at Alexandria, to receive letters which had
been addressed to him by Pope Damasus. The posi-

[1] See Dr. Swainson's important work on the *Creeds of the
Church*.

tion and authority of Athanasius must have been held in lofty esteem, and his own consciousness of it is seen in the criticism he proffers on certain proceedings of the bishop and synods of Rome.

Athanasius, in the year 368, began to rebuild the Cæsarean church which had been burned in the reign of Julian, and in 369 commenced the erection of another church in Alexandria, which was afterwards called by his own name. The old tree had struck deep roots, and the whole of the Eastern Church rejoiced in the shadow of it.

During this period we have several side-lights thrown upon the character of Athanasius and the state of the churches. One of these gleams of light arises from the superiority of the great leader to mere canonical rule, when common sense came into conflict with ecclesiastical precedent. In the district of Pentapolis, an aged bishop, Philo, independently of any consultation with Athanasius and by his own authority, had yielded to the desire of two small townships, and consecrated to the episcopate over them a young layman, Siderius by name. An outcry was made against this double violation of usage, but Athanasius was convinced from what he heard of young Siderius that he would discharge the episcopal functions wisely, and he not only left him in peace, but ultimately transferred him to a position of much greater influence and importance at Ptolemais.

Another event evinced his stern sense of righteousness. It came to his knowledge that one of the imperial governors of Libya had been guilty of gross and glaring sin, and he did not hesitate to excommunicate him from all church privileges and to forbid all communion with him on the part of the faithful. Amongst other churches which doubtless received the sentence that had been pronounced upon the governor, Basil, the Archbishop of New Cæsarea, accepted them, and wrote the first of a series of letters to Athanasius. In this letter (numbered 47 in some editions—60 in the *Benedictine*) Basil expresses his abhorrence of the offence committed and his approval of the sentence, and promises to have it observed throughout his diocese. It might seem that the unhappy man had received some appointment in Cappadocia. Basil writes to Athanasius with extreme reverence as to the one man who, acquainted with the condition of the churches far and near, might be able, by his counsel and prayers, to bring order and harmony into the distracted Church of Antioch. Basil evidently leaned to the side of Meletius, and lamented the position of Paulinus, and felt persuaded that the immense weight of character and office sustained by Athanasius could compose the schism between them. He wished that Athanasius could convene a general synod with the assistance of the Bishop of Rome, to discuss this public scandal. If this were impossible, Basil besought Athanasius to visit the Eastern Church in person, or to send adequate representatives of his views. Age and infirmity rendered it impossible for Athanasius to comply with the request, but he seems to have done his utmost to compose the difference.

He had taken in 363 a very decided part in this controversy, and would find it very difficult to withdraw his confidence from Paulinus. Some think that he did become reconciled to Meletius, or Meletius to him; but we are not certain of the result of his well-meant endeavour in the interests of peace.

From our present standpoint it is especially interesting to learn from this incident the vast place filled by Athanasius in the opinions of his contemporaries, and the credit given to the great controversialist as the triumphant peace-maker. A further incident establishes the same reputation, for another difficulty arose in the mind of Basil with reference to the wide-spread diffusion in the East of the teaching of Marcellus—that old friend of Athanasius, on whose eccentricities he had often looked with a very lenient eye. Athanasius had indeed, without mentioning his name, discussed and condemned (in *Oratio* iv., *c. Arianos*) views attributed to Marcellus; but now, according to the great Basil, these speculations were as prevalent, and as adverse to the truth, as those of Arius, not only tending to Sabellianism and to the virtual absorption of the Son in the Father, but to the terminable character of the glory and kingdom of the Christ. Marcellus heard of the letter addressed to Athanasius by Basil, and made haste to lay before his old friend and fellow-sufferer, by the lips of certain faithful representatives, the doctrines he had been advocating. The issue of the discussion was that they and the Egyptian bishops hit upon an *eirenicon,* and confessed together the eternity of the Son and personal Word of God, and together repudiated the Sabellianism with which Marcellus had been charged.

Dr. Bright observes 'that if his final opinion of Marcellus was lenient, he was far from tolerating in the latter years of his life any theories which seemed heterodox respecting the human side of the incarnation.' In letters still extant we find Athanasius holding with great firmness and clearness the three positions—(1) that the Christ was perfect God, sharing in all the glory and essence of the Father; and (2) perfect Man, having assumed humanity in all its fulness and completeness; and (3) that the union between the Divinity and Humanity was so absolute that there was one Christ, and there were not two Christs. He justified the worship of the manhood because of the *one Person* of the Christ. He condemned the virtual *denial* of His humanity that was involved in the supposition that the eternal Word took the place of the human soul or spirit in the person of Christ. His very latest work, three books against the *Apollinarians,* written in 372, reveals the same grasp of thought, a similar breadth of apprehension, the like extraordinary tenacity of hold, and the same childlike dependence on Scripture which had characterized his earlier writings. It is not to be supposed that he would have stood all the tests applied by the orthodox when the controversies of the fifth and sixth centuries had run their course; but he displayed so keen a sense of the central truth of the incarnation, that one might easily imagine him holding at once the *via media* between the Monophysite sects on the one side and Nestorians on the other. Thus he lays the greatest emphasis on the veritable humanity of the Lord, enumerating all its phases, and he will not admit that this humanity 'came down from heaven,' but urges that it was born into the world: nor will he grant that we adore His humanity except as united to the eternal Word. He shows by numerous quotations from the Gospel that the flesh of Christ was not consubstantial with the Father, and that the Divinity was not *per se* the subject of either suffering or death, except as united *to* and *in* the humanity of Christ.

We cannot say with entire certainty whether the death of this noble confessor and lifelong martyr of the faith occurred in the year 371 or 373. The majority of the best and latest authorities decide for the latter date, and do not place it earlier than the month of May. The turmoil of conflict in the Church had not ceased; many were suffering from the hard and cruel policy of the Arians; the secular power was continuously interfering with the action of the Church and with the office of its chief pastors; but the cyclone which raged around the Mediterranean shores left an almost preternatural calm over the closing days of one who, though he had nominally held the bishopric of Alexandria for forty-six years, had been five times cruelly dismissed from his see under the insults and wrongs which have been recounted. He never relaxed his maintenance of the grand truth which he held to be vital to the Christian faith; and after a lifetime of toil and anxiety he passed away amid the tears and love of his own people. He named as his successor one of the companions of his wanderings who was well versed in the ideas and principles which had governed his own life. Peter was accepted by the bishops of Egypt, and solemnly consecrated to the vacant see; though this step had hardly been taken when the sleeping foes arose and, under the leadership of Lucius the Arian, renewed their tactics and their appeals to physical force, and for a while bade fair to make the career of Peter as chequered and disturbed as that of his illustrious predecessor.

The Festal letters, which Athanasius produced year after year at Easter, reflect the deeper and tenderer aspects of his religious character, and show that he was set upon the cultivation of the Divine life, and held that orthodox doctrine was but a means to a noble and sublime end.

A few sentences from these seem to us the appropriate cerements in which to embalm his holy memory. Thus, in 329, he wrote: 'Let us keep the feast on the first day of the week, as a symbol of the world to come, in which we here receive a pledge that we shall have hereafter everlasting life. Then having passed from hence, we shall keep a perfect feast with Christ, while we cry out, like the saints, "I will pass to the place of the wondrous tabernacle, to the house of God; with the voice of gladness and thanksgiving, the shouting of those that rejoice; so that sorrow and affliction and sighing shall flee away, and gladness and joy be upon our heads!"'

After recounting the condescension of our Lord in washing His disciples' feet, he wrote: 'How shall we sufficiently admire the lovingkindness of our Saviour? We should not only bear His image, but receive from Him a pattern of heavenly conversation, that suffering we should not threaten, and in everything commit ourselves to God who judgeth righteously!' Again in 329 he wrote: 'Christ our Passover is sacrificed, so that all of us, contemplating the eternity of the Word, may have nearness of access to Him. What else is the feast but the service of the soul? What is that service but prolonged prayer and unceasing thanksgiving?'

In 333 he wrote: 'It is God, my beloved, who brought about the slaying of His Son for our salvation, and gave us the reason for this holy feast. He made the world free by the blood of our Saviour, and opened the gates of heaven, granting through our Saviour an uninterrupted way for those who ascend thereto.' Well might one say, 'What shall I render unto the Lord for all He has done unto me!' for 'instead of death he received life, freedom instead of bondage, and the kingdom of heaven instead of the grave! We imitate the deeds of saints when we acknowledge Him who died, and no longer live unto ourselves.'

These letters are one ceaseless call for repentance, purity, love to God and man, and perpetual reminder that in the days which we commemorate, the Lord suffered in our stead, and summoned us to a full consecration. 'The Lord,' said he, 'regarded our salvation as a delight and a peculiar gain, and looked upon our destruction as His loss.' Year after year he called upon his brethren for holy living, because Christ our Passover is sacrificed for us. He taught them to enter into the joy of the Lord. In one of his very latest words he wrote : ' He that sitteth upon the cherubim, having appeared with greater grace and lovingkindness, led into Paradise with Himself the confessing thief, and, having entered heaven as our Forerunner, opened the gates to all.' After quoting the whole of Heb. xii. 18–22, he added: ' Who would not wish to enjoy high companionship with these ! Who does not desire to be enrolled with these, that he may hear with them, " Come, ye blessed of My Father, inherit the kingdom prepared for you from the foundation of the world ? " ' These Festal letters may be compared with the *Imitation of Christ*, in their unaffected piety, their freedom from controversy, their burning love to the Incarnate God, their practical wisdom and abounding charity.

CHAPTER XV.

THE CHARACTER OF ATHANASIUS.

'The life of Athanasius,' as Mohler observed, 'is his best panegyric.' But few men in the history of the world, and a smaller proportion still of professed theologians, have received more abundant or less grudging tributes to their personal excellence and nobility of character. He was hated and persecuted for half a century with all the weapons of envy, malice and wilful misrepresentation; and he had the power of exciting the bitter animosity of courtiers like Eusebius of Nicomedia, and worldly self seekers like Ursacius and Valens. A succession of Roman emperors feared and resented his independence. Even Constantine the Great found the will of Athanasius more than a match for his own, and for State purposes lent his supreme power to those who were thirsting for the degradation of the greatest man then living. Constantius revealed all the littleness and baseness of a vacillating and petulant nature in his endeavour to curb and crush the personal influence of Athanasius. He was honoured by the peculiar hatred and murderous indignation of Julian, and his closing years were embittered by the venomous wrath of the Eastern Emperor Valens.

The Arian chiefs had reason to dread the man who with the hand of a master could not only expose their insincerities and their craving for influence, but lay bare the schemes and plots of their fertile brains, and who, after having been mainly instrumental in affirming the faith of the Church in the Unity of God, held the absolute Deity of the Son of God to be incarnated in the Lord Jesus Christ,—who further proved by arguments, which ultimately seemed irresistible to a Greek mind, that in the endless shifts by which the Arians professed to establish the supremacy of the Father they were endangering the greatest truth of revelation, alike depriving Almighty God of His essential nature and dishonouring the Saviour of the world.

Doubtless among many groups of semi-Arians and Anomæans there were men entirely honest to their convictions and enthusiastic worshippers and servants of the Lord Jesus Christ; nor must we disregard the missionary and evangelistic fervour of such saints as Ulphilas—one of the earliest translators of Scripture into any Gothic language,—nor underrate the courage and tolerant spirit of a ruler like Theodoric the Ostrogoth; but we can never forget the loathsome hypocrisies, nor sufficiently condemn the crafty methods by which the Arian chiefs endeavoured to serve their purpose. Not one, but many holy men were cruelly accused of impossible offences, and were removed from their pastorates by these unscrupulous men, apparently for no other reason than for their adhesion to doctrine which they did not dare themselves to repudiate openly.

Of these sufferers Athanasius was the most conspicuous example. Certainly he had the faculty of exciting the animosity and evoking the malign conspiracies of a succession of ecclesiastics during the forty-six years of his nominal occupancy of the see of Alexandria. It is moreover certain that some of those who positively agreed with his doctrine were so swayed by the ceaseless iteration of the disproved and even perfectly refuted calumnies that they were at times deceived into condemnation of his person and tempted to dispossess him of his rights. All that was mean and sycophantic shrank from him in disgust and fear. Coarse natures, like those of George or Gregory, felt towards him as the wolf feels to the lamb. The suppressed pagans, the barely tolerated Jews, and the Neoplatonic flatterers of Julian felt instinctive recoil from his ideas, and from the power with which he proclaimed them. We have also seen that he could strike fire with every sweep of his *Excalibur*, that he did not mince his words when in the thick of a fight, that he used language valiant and violent in exposing the fallacy of an argument or the baseness of an intrigue, and he may at times have exaggerated the deviations of his opponents from Biblical truth. He was a very human man after all.

But on the other hand few men have rejoiced in a wider chorus of panegyric or more devoted 'troops of friends.' We have seen that distinguished men like the Bishops Marcellus and Eustathius, the Popes Julius and Liberius; confessors and martyrs like Paphnutius and Potammon; ascetics like the great Anthony, the aged Hosius, the thoughtful Hilary, and the fiery Lucifer were ready to encounter and suffer much, not only out of faithfulness to Catholic doctrine, but out of chivalrous belief in the honour, the virtue, the purity and moral goodness of Athanasius. The monks of a hundred monasteries were ready to die for him; the bulk of the population of his native city, notwithstanding cruel wrongs done to them for their constancy, were ready time after time to welcome him back with transports of enthusiasm.

Some of the characteristics which gave him this hold may be reviewed.

1. The courage which he manifested.—The emperors of the world, vast assemblages of hostile bishops, the drilled soldiers and clever detectives of the army did not daunt him. Years of wandering in burning deserts did not subdue his energy. He maintained his idea of truth *contra mundum*,—' against the world' in arms; he maintained his integrity with the fervour of Job and the bravery of Socrates. Nevertheless—

2. His self-oblation was conspicuous.—He offered up himself continually for the good of others and for the great cause enshrined in his person His self-mortification astonished the monks of the Nitrian desert, and commended the monastic life to the cooler brain and larger outlook of the Teuton and the Gaul. If he fled in mysterious fashion from the persecutors who thirsted for his blood, it was because, humanly speaking, no other way seemed open for him to preserve the palladium entrusted to his care. The flight was, moreover, into the desolation of the wilderness, and to face not only the misery of espionage and search, but severest toil and travail.

3. He was remarkable for clearness and lucidity of mind and astonishing power of expression —He was no rhetorician. His periods cannot be compared with those of Libanius or Gregory, Chrysostom or Basil; but there is in them condensed wisdom and clear-cut utterance which leave the reader in no doubt about his meaning; and his wise and rapid judgments on men and movements, and on the best steps which were possible in difficult complications, made him a born leader. His consecration of Frumentius as Bishop of Auxume in Ethiopia, his advice to Dracontius, his acceptance of the uncanonically ordained Bishop Siderius, his

adroitness in rebutting the charge of the murder of Arsenius, his appeals to Constantine, and his Apology to Constantius, gleam with the sprightliness and clearness of his vision. He could turn aside the sharp weapons of his enemies, and cut through whole coils of red tape with his mother-wit.

4. A certain cloud of romance encircled him.—A power went forth from him which transmuted commonplace into charm, and gave an astonishing and dramatic effect to the crises of his life. The encounter with Constantine in his own city, the tragic and pathetic scene in the Church of St. Theonas, and his escapes from capture in the third, fourth, and fifth exiles, almost suggest a supernatural and legendary colouring. If they were not avouched by unusually powerful testimony, they would read like chapters of enchantment. His enemies were closeted with empresses, and complotted with the eunuchs and chamberlains of the court. The Dukes of Egypt and prefects of the city so feared his moral power as to tremble for their own. Philosophers and satirists were against him; but by some mysterious magic he outwitted emperors and patriarchs, Arians and apostates. 'Only' (as Hooker said) 'of Athanasius there was nothing observed through the long tragedy other than such as it became a wise man to do and a righteous to suffer. So that this was the plain condition of those times: the whole world against Athanasius, and Athanasius against it. Half a hundred years spent in doubtful trial, which of the two in the end would prevail,—the side which had all, or else the part which had no friend but God and death'?

5. The inflexible purpose of the man.—'We have,' (said Gibbon) 'seldom an opportunity of observing,

either in active or speculative life, what effect may be produced or what obstacles may be surmounted by the force of a single mind when it is inflexibly applied to the pursuit of a single object. The immortal name of Athanasius will never be separated from the Catholic Doctrine of the Trinity to whose defence he consecrated every moment and faculty of his being.' This fundamental aim dominated every other. It appears in the earliest of his writings and crowns the latest of them. He felt the overwhelming greatness, the transcendent and august majesty of the only God to such an intense degree that every deviation in thought from it hurt him like a wound. He had seen the most stupendous displays of the splendour of the lords many and gods many of heathendom; but the gay procession and solemn mystery were, in his sight, treason to the supreme majesty of Him in whom we live, move and have our being.

Nevertheless he adored the One God in the Person of the Lord, who had saved him from Nature-worship and delivered him from sin and death. He felt, he knew, that Jesus Christ was Lord of all, that as Son of God and Son of man, and Redeemer of the world, He was in the midst of the throne. From his childhood he had thought of the Son of God incarnated as so entirely One with the Father that he honoured the Son even as he honoured the Father. When he found men attempting by endless word-splittings to deny the Divine attributes of the Son, and to give Him the rank of a creature, he saw himself at the edge of an inclined plane which sloped off rapidly into the abysses of polytheism, and his recoil therefrom almost carried him back to a merely subjective treatment of the difference between the reality of the Father and Son. Indeed, it must be admitted that he was always more lenient to Sabellian departures from than to Arian repudiations of the great faith.

His principal arguments were drawn, not from the decisions of councils, nor from the dogmas of great churchmen, but from the teaching of the Holy Scriptures. He must have known these by heart, and could on occasion summon testimonies from every book of the Old and New Testaments to confirm his exegesis of particular passages. Every vindication of his own character against the absurd, reckless, and refutable calumnies of his enemies seemed entirely subordinate to the testimony he was bound to bear to the Divinity of the Redeemer. He exposed the sophistries of his enemies with dexterous logic and persuasive argument; and though at times with heart-breaking and disastrous issues to himself, yet practically he won the victory. Nicene doctrine became the platform on which all the subsequent controversies touching the *person* of Christ were wrought out.

6. Yet Athanasius revealed a profound sympathy with the difficulties felt by those who could not accept his terms, and even hesitated to adopt such a fundamental word as 'homoousios.' He dealt most graciously with men like Basil of Ancyra, who accepted the principle, but refused the Shibboleth of the Catholic orthodoxy. In the same way, he tenderly mediated between those who, though they were holding identical doctrine, had been confused by the double use of the word 'hypostasis.' He had gentle words for Liberius and Hosius, who, after suffering imprisonment and exile for their confidence in him, had given way at last under a great pressure of temptation. Even the eccentric and erratic Marcellus is more genially handled by Athanasius than by any of his contemporaries. His meekness in the hour of Julian's madness against

him reminds us of Stephen's dying words. At first he strove to minimize the difference from the Catholic faith of the elder Apollinarians. He sought to reconcile the adverse interests of Meletius and Paulinus at Antioch, and to soften the position of those who had during the Arian persecution succumbed to the imperious will of the notorious Gregory or George. In the heat of high debate he could hit hard and use strong words of condemnation; but when he returned to his see he was singularly devoid of vindictive feeling. Though at intervals he wielded an almost imperial sway over the entire provinces of Upper and Lower Egypt, he was noble and sympathetic in his occupancy of 'the evangelical throne.'

7. Lastly, his piety towards God, his devout and humble life, his adoring gratitude to the Saviour from sin and the Victor of death, and his grand hope for the world, his profound relish for prayer and the holy communion, his humility, his confession of sin, the chastening of his heart in remembrance of the broken body and shed blood of the Son of man, reveal a profound Christian consciousness, the image and memory of which the Church of Christ will 'not willingly let die.'

The extraordinary eulogium of Gregory of Nazianzus has been frequently referred to in the foregoing pages; but, as Tillemont observed, it would be a limitless task to collect that which others have said to his honour and renown. Epiphanius gave him the title of 'the Father of the Orthodox Faith.' Lucifer declared that 'one sees in him the perfect ideal of justice realized.' Cyril declared that 'all the world did homage to the purity and holiness of his teaching, and that he had filled the world with the fragrant odour of his writings.

Testimonies without end may be brought from Augustine and Fulgentius, to Luther, Calvin and Hooker. The Church historians, from Baronius to Neander, resound his praise. Milman, Cardinal Newman, Dean Stanley, Mohler, de Broglie, Montalembert, Villemain, and Fialon, are pronounced in their appreciation. Even Gibbon almost achieves an eulogy when reviewing the labour and heroism of 'the immortal Athanasius'; and Mr. Fiske, one of the latest disciples of Herbert Spencer, gives a higher place to St. Athanasius in the genesis and formulation of the idea of God than to any other Father of the Christian Church.

TABLE OF DATES.

The following table of the dates of the chief events in the life of Athanasius is adopted by Mr. Gwatkin, and endorsed with some queries by Archdeacon Farrar.

	A D
Birth of Athanasius	297
Persecution under Maximian	303
Writes *c. Gentes* and *De Incarnatione*	318
Excommunication of Arius	321
Council of Nicæa	325
Election of Athanasius	326 or 328
Council of Tyre	August, 335
Council of Jerusalem	September, 335
Athanasius at Constantinople	October, 335
Exile of Athanasius	February, 336
Death of Arius	336
Death of Constantine	May, 337
Return of Athanasius	November, 337
Athanasius expelled by Philagrius	339
Council at Rome Letter of Julius	340
Council of Dedication at Antioch	341
Death of Eusebius of Nicomedia	342
Councils of Sardica and Philippopolis	343
Macrostich Creed, Antioch	344
Death of Gregory of Alexandria	345
The Second Return of Athanasius	346
The Death of Constans	350
Council of Arles	353
Exile of Hosius and Liberius	355
Athanasius driven into Wilderness	356
Composes *Apolog ad Const* and *pro Fuga*	356
The Four Discourses—*Hist. Arian*	358
The Dated Creed of Sirmium	359
Councils of Rimini and Seleucia	359
Athanasius writes *De Synodis*	359
Death of Constantius	361
Murder of George, Third Return of Athanasius	362
Fourth Exile, Fourth Return	363
Fifth Exile and Return	366
Death of Athanasius	373

INDEX.

Acacius at Rimini, 123, victory of, 126.
Aetius, a leader of extreme Arians, 117.
Ædesius, story of, 41.
Alexander, Bishop of Alexandria, recognises orders of Athanasius, 22, death of, 39.
Alexander founds Alexandria, 10.
Alexandria, foundation of, 10, buildings of, 10, Pharos, 11, Greek quarter, 11, library, 12, Egyptian quarter, 13, condition of, 13, persecutions in, 14, controversies in, 17-21, Neoplatonic speculations at, 26, persecutions at, 65, churches of, 86, massacre at, 88, cruelties in, 134.
Anomæans, opinions of the, 118, plan of, 121.
Antinoe, 158
Anthony, life of, not written by Athanasius, 24, story of, 55, influence of, on Augustine, 55.
Apollinarians, opinions of the, 149.
Arcaph, John, brings false charges against Athanasius, 45
Arians, plots of the, 83, treachery of, 89, cruelties of, 94, divisions among 116-127.
Arius, life and character of, 25, views of, 26, his appearance, 27, writes *Thalia*, 27, Gregory of Nyssa on influence of, 28, excommunicated at Alexandria, 28, banished, 35, death of, 58.
Arsenius, supposed murder of, 45; brought before Council at Tyre, 48.
Artemius, Duke, story of, 96
Athanasius, birth of, 21, legend as to his youthful consecration, 22, his mind and character, 22; writes *Against the Gentiles* and *Concerning the Incarnation*, 23, his classical knowledge, 24, not author of *Life of Anthony*, 24, at Council of Nicæa, 30, succeeds Alexander, 40, consecrates Frumentius, 42, opposed by Meletians, 44, summoned to Nicomedia, 44, charges against him, 44, his voyage on the Nile, 46, refuses to attend council at Cæsarea, 47, appears at Tyre, 47, appeals to Emperor, 50, his interview with Constantine, 50, charged with treason, 51, exiled, 52, at Trèves, 54; his influence there, 54, on death of Arius, 60, date of his release from Treves, 62, his arrival at Alexandria, 63, charges against, 63, deposed by council at Antioch, 65; goes to Rome, 65, writes *Encyclical Epistle*, 65, deposed by second synod at Antioch, 69, acquitted by Sardican Bishops, 72, return of, 73, writes *Concerning Dionysius, Apology, Against the Arians, Syllogus, Nicene Definition of the Faith*, 77, sends envoys to the Emperor, 78; summoned to Milan, 78, his *Apology to Constantius*, 80, 86, writes *Epistola ad Dracontium*, 81, treacherous and cruel conduct to, of Duke Syrianus, 87, consecrates the Cæsareum, 86, third exile, 88, his supposed hiding-places, 90, his *Apology for Flight*, 92, his *Arian History, Encyclical Epistle, Letter to Serapion, Four Discourses against the Arians*, 95; his fascinating powers, 96, his *Divinity of the Holy Spirit*, 127, again returns to Alexandria, 139; his noble conduct, 140, influence of his ministry, 153, his flight, 155; his voyage on the Nile, and narrow escape, 156, in the Thebaid, 157,

INDEX

again returns to Alexandria, 160; his interview with Jovian, 160, his citation of Nicene Creed, 161, at Antioch, 162, again escapes, 167, recalled, 168, the *Canon of Athanasius*, 169, *Expositio Fidei*, 171, *Creed of Athanasius*, 171, *De Incarnatione*, *Epistle to the Africans*, 172 rebuilds the Cæsareum Church, 173, conduct concerning Siderius, 173, correspondence with Basil, 174, his opinions, 175, his death, 176, his *Festal Letter*, 177, character of, 180, his enemies, 181, his friends, 182, his courage, self-oblation, clearness and wit, 183, romance of, 184, his inflexibility, 184, his sympathy, 186, his piety, 187, eulogiums of, 187

Augustine, influence of *Life of Anthony* on, 55

Axum or Auxume, Frumentius at, 41

Basil of Ancyra, surrender of semi-Arian position, 120.

Basil of New Cæsarea, letters to Athanasius, 174, on opinions of Marcellus, 175

Cæsareum, the, consecration of, 86

Canon of Athanasius, the, analysis of, 169

Canons of Antioch, the, 68

Church of the Holy Sepulchre, dedication of, 56.

Constans, death of, 75

Constantine at Council of Nicæa, 29, vacillation of, 35, his interview with Athanasius, 50, sends Athanasius into exile, 52, his interview with Arius, 59, his death, 60, character of, 61

Constantine the Younger, letter of, 52, his friendliness to Athanasius, 54

Constantius becomes emperor, 60, completes Church of the Holy Sepulchre, 68, calls Council of Sardica, 70, his letters to Athanasius, 73, becomes sole ruler, 76, suddenly changes his mind, 76, calls Athanasius to Milan, 78, calls council at Arles, 79, makes Julian *Cæsar*, 80, duplicity of, 88, his hatred of Athanasius, 91, calls a council at Rimini, 121, death of, 132

Council at Antioch deposes Athanasius, and appoints Gregory of Cappadocia, 65, second synod at, 63, deposes Athanasius, 69.

Council at Arles, 79.

Council at Cæsarea, 47.

Council at Nicæa, Constantine at, 29, delegates at, 29, Athanasius at, 30, creed of, 30-32, Eusebians at, 31, conflict at, 36, decisions as to Meletius, 38

Council at Rimini, proceedings at, 121-127.

Council at Sardica, 70, conduct of, 71

Councils at Sirmium and at Philippopolis, 77, 118, 119

Council at Tyre, proceedings of, 47-50 (*see* Synods).

Creed of Athanasius, the, 32, 171

Creed of Nicæa, 32

Dated Creed, the, 121.

De Incarnatione, the, 172, analysis of, 23.

De Synodis, analysis of, 125.

Diogenes, mission of, 87

Dionysius of Alexandria, his opinions, 20

Dionysius of Rome, his opinions, 21.

Divinity of the Holy Spirit, analysis of, 127

Dracontius, story of, 81

Ethiopian Church, story of foundation of, 41.

Eunomius, opinions of, 117

Eusebius, party of, at Nicæa, 31; refuses to sign creed, and is exiled, 35, recall of, 40, opposes Eustathius, 43, and Athanasius, 44, perjury of, 52, tactics of party of, at Jerusalem and Constantinople, 57, their treachery, 63, hold a council at Antioch, 64

Eusebius of Vercellæ, return of, 141

Eustathius, charges against, 43.

Expositio Fidei, the, 171

Festal Letters, extracts from, 177

Four Discourses against the Arians, analysis of, 99, the first, 101, the second, 109, the third, 112, the fourth, 114

Frumentius, story of, 41.

Galerius, persecution under, 16

George of Cappadocia, character of, 93; cruelties of, 93, violence of, 133, his death, 134

Gregory of Cappadocia appointed to succeed Athanasius, 65.

Gregory of Nazianzus, on return of Athanasius to Alexandria, 63

Gregory of Nyssa, on influence of Arius, 28.

Gwatkin, Mr, on style of Athanasius, 125, on Constantine, 61.

Hermopolis, 158

Hilary of Poictiers, charges against, 83.

INDEX.

Holy Spirit, the, opinions concerning, 142
Homæan party, the, tactics of, 122
Homoousion, controversy concerning, 31, 36
Hosius of Cordova, plot against, 84
Hypostasis, meaning of the term, 145
Ischyras, story of, 44
Jerusalem, dedication of Church of Holy Sepulchre at, 56
Jews, belief in Unity of the Godhead, 17.
Jovian becomes emperor, 160, his letters to Athanasius, 160, asks instruction in the faith, 160, his interview with Athanasius, 160, his death, 162
Julian, becomes *Cæsar*, 80, character of, 129, personal appearance of, 130, becomes a pagan, 131, victories of, 132, becomes sole emperor, 133, his letter on the death of George, 134, his edicts of indulgence, 136, aims of, 137 his anger against Athanasius, 153, orders his exile, 154, writes the *Cæsars* and the *Misapogon*, 157, his death, 159
Julius, Pope, Eusebian, appeal to, 64, his reception of Athanasius, 66, his letter, 66, death of, 78.
Liberius becomes Bishop of Rome, 78, plot against, 84, fall, 92, 119
Lucifer, rage of, 180, return of, 141
Macarius, charges against, 44
Macrostich, the, or 'the Long-lined Confession,' 70.
Magnentius, usurpation of, 75
Marcellus of Ancyra, charges against, 57, opinions of, 58, an *euchnocon* found, 175.
Meletians, community of, 44.
Meletius, conduct and opinions of, 38.
Meropius, story of 41
Neoplatonic speculations at Alexandria, 26
Nicodemia, earthquake at, 121.
Origen, opinions of, 20
Pachomius, modesty of, 46.
Pammon visited by Athanasius, 158.
Paphnutius at Tyre, 49.

Paulinus, firmness of, 79
Persecutions, 15, 65, 89, 93
Person, meaning of the word, 145.
Pharos, the, at Alexandria, 11
Philagrius, cruelties of, 65
Philo the Jew, his method of interpretation, 18
Philippopolis, schismatic council at, 71
Pistus, consecration of, 64
Potomiæna, death of, 14.
Potammon, at Tyre, 49, death of, 65
Rufinus, his story of consecration of Athanasius, 22, of Frumentius, 41.
Sabellius, his opinions, 19
Secundus consecrates Pistus, 64.
Semi-Arians, the, 177.
Siderius, conduct of Athanasius concerning, 173
Sotadean metre, the influence of, 28
Stanley, Dean, on character of Constantine, 61
Synods at Alexandria, 64, 141.
Synod at Ancyra, 119
Synod at Antioch, 162.
Synod at Constantinople, 57
Synod at Jerusalem, Eusebian tactics at, 57
Synod at Milan, 70, 83 (*see* Councils).
Syrianus, conduct of, 87.
Thalia, the, of Arius, 27.
Theognis at Council of Nicæa, 35, recall of, 40, opposes Eustathius, 43, Athanasius, 44
Trèves, description of, 52, Athanasius at, 54
Ursacius, submission of, 74; again recants, 76, holds a synod at Sirmium, 118, at Rimini, 122
Valentinian becomes emperor, 162, appoints Valens emperor, 163.
Valens, Bishop, submission of, 74, again recants, 76, holds a synod at Sirmium, 118, at Rimini, 122
Valens becomes emperor, 163, his opinions, 163, his edict against Athanasius, 164, permits his recall, 167.
Vetranio, usurpation of, 75

www.ingramcontent.com/pod-product-compliance
Lightning Source LLC
Chambersburg PA
CBHW071423160426
43195CB00013B/1780